MW00773936

THE CORONAVIRUS PANDEMIC

*A Global Wake-Up Call to
Change and Redeem Lives*

ESMAT M. GABRIEL

ISBN 978-1-63961-529-2 (paperback)
ISBN 978-1-63961-531-5 (hardcover)
ISBN 978-1-63961-530-8 (digital)

Copyright © 2022 by Esmat M. Gabriel

All rights reserved. No part of this publication may be reproduced, distributed, or transmitted in any form or by any means, including photocopying, recording, or other electronic or mechanical methods without the prior written permission of the publisher. For permission requests, solicit the publisher via the address below.

Christian Faith Publishing
832 Park Avenue
Meadville, PA 16335
www.christianfaithpublishing.com

The scripture quotations contained in this book are from the New King James Version, copyright © 1982 by Thomas Nelson, Inc., and are used by permission. Any mistakes and all opinions in this book are entirely my own. The writer and publisher are grateful to the foregoing and those others whose materials, whether in the public domain or protected by copyright, are cited throughout this book. Other than minor conventional edits for clarity, the excerpts used in this work have been transcribed verbatim. If any copyrighted materials have been inadvertently used in this work without proper credit being given in one form or another, please notify the publisher in writing so that future printings of this work may be corrected accordingly.

Printed in the United States of America

To the family of Saints Mary and Joseph
To whom these words are dedicated.
May this book grant those who read it
The path that leads to a holy life.

✝

To Fr. & Mrs. David Buch
With Love
Ernest & Joan Gabriel
Feb. 12, 2023

Contents

BOOK TWO
GREAT CHARACTER TRANSFORMATION

BOOK THREE
THE EFFECTS OF FAMILY VALUES
ON *ENJOYABLE FAMILY LIFE*

Acknowledgments

I would be hard-pressed to think of an author who needed more help and received it in greater measure than I did in the writing of this book. First and foremost, I would like to thank my wife, Irene, and both of my daughters, Mary and Amy, who encouraged me to continue writing. They wanted me to never stop speaking about divine intervention to bolster humanity against fear, and to proclaim that these challenging times, when viewed from a historical perspective, are blessed times. These are times in which man is bearing increasing witness to the mandate to love our brothers and sisters as ourselves.

But we cannot love unless we know that every man is our brother and every woman, our sister. And we cannot know that until we are ready to admit that God is our Father. He is our greatest source of hope, even as we are blessed by the power of science promising life-saving vaccines to solve the pandemic challenge. As I undertook this important and urgent task, I am especially grateful to my wife for her devotion to this undertaking and her invaluable review of the manuscript. Her excellent suggestions, care, and sensitivity enabled me to really focus not only on the writing of this book but my previous publication as well.

In addition, I feel a deep sense of gratitude to the following:

- My wife, Irene, for her insights and purity of soul that are blessings to our life. She is my constant and unshakable support.
- My daughters, Mary and Amy, for living lives of integrity and service and who strive to subjugate their will to God's will. It is easy to teach principles to loved ones who live by those principles themselves.

- My proactive publication specialist, Kristy Bilski, at Christian Faith Publishing (CFP) for her promptness and diligence. Her cooperation has been key to effective communication with the working team that made all the difference.
- The professional team at CFP for their creative artistic designs and production help.

Preface

Much of the content of this book was first delivered in Coptic Orthodox churches, at Coptic youth assemblies and Sunday school gatherings, and at Coptic family conferences in the United States and Canada. When the coronavirus pandemic arrived, my plans suddenly came to a halt, and I no longer could engage in new speech commitments. Nonetheless, I continued to write about subjects and events of significant importance to family life during this time of social distancing and self-isolation.

Regretfully, there appears to be no end in sight to this global disaster, at least for the time being. According to Johns Hopkins University as reported by CNN on May 22, 2020, the number of cases reached 5.1 million worldwide, including over 333,000 deaths. By March 17, 2021, the *New York Times* reported the coronavirus had spread to nearly every country, sickened more than 80 million people, and killed at least 1.7 million. By February 9, 2022, the worldwide coronavirus cases reached 402,353,264 and deaths 5,786,222 as recorded by worldometers.info/coronavirus.

In America, the majority of people thought they could continue to travel anywhere they wanted and enjoy all the customary pleasures available to them. According to St. Augustine, "We 'have all we want' is a terrible saying when 'all' does not include God. We find God an interruption… God wants to give us something, but cannot, because our hands are full—there's nowhere for Him to put it."

For the first time in history, churches are empty and services are now being held online only. Attendance at essential services like funerals and weddings is limited only to immediate family. This has never happened before the Holy Week (known as the Holy Pascha, or "Passover," week) in the Coptic Orthodox Church. Celebrations in

2020 were disrupted not only in the United States but in every church around the world. One exception was in Coptic Orthodox monasteries, where monks had the opportunity to enjoy the traditional beauty and spiritual depth of the passion week inside their churches.

During the Holy Week, Copts celebrate that the Lord has given them life by defeating death. They truly rejoice in the life-giving mystery of His death, burial, and resurrection. Coptic Orthodox services are usually at their peak at this time, and members have special devotion, love, and fidelity to spend the Pascha week within the bosom of their local churches. During the pandemic, millions of Copts were still able to participate in prayers from wherever they were in the world—thanks to communication tools such as Zoom—but it was not the same. As the world began shutting down, places that were once full of people, life, and activities became ghost towns due to massive restrictions. Business and school closures, travel restrictions, and bans on groups and community gathering became the new reality.

It is indeed a sad, painful reality to hundreds of millions of people in the United States and around the world. The prolific spiritual writer C. S. Lewis once wrote, "We can ignore even pleasure. But pain insists upon being attended to. God whispers to us in our pleasures, speaks in our conscience, but shouts in our pains: it is his megaphone to rouse a deaf world." Pain is like a siren going off; something is wrong, whether it's physical pain, emotional pain, or spiritual pain. Yet pain and suffering what moves the heart of God as we see Him act with compassion throughout the Gospel to alleviate pain and restore people's health and well-being.

During the seclusion imposed by the coronavirus, I attempted to proceed in the face of this "invisible enemy" and strived to undertake a worthwhile task. I decided it was time to put in writing what I had said at the microphone for years. The only thing missing is the passion that goes a long way when speaking to an audience, the ability to emphasize a word or a concept through inflection and tone of voice. Giving a speech before a live audience gives the opportunity to champion the subject and cause that I care about most. Needless to say, the topic that I aspire to speak about is education and how it benefits the whole man—mind, soul, and spirit.

In rewriting these presentations, I found myself either updating or deleting parts of them due to newly acquired information and a better understanding of the subject. I have spent decades in my profession cultivating the truth that man is created in the image of his Creator. Man is naturally good; what has corrupted us from this state is parting company from our Creator and/or denying His existence altogether.

My role during my educational career and clinical practice has mainly been teaching and treating others. I worked within universities, scientific societies, youth organizations, mental health systems, and religious communities. The mission set before me now is mainly for a higher humanitarian purpose. It is to alleviate human suffering and teach new generations of health professionals to passionately commit to improving the life of man—mind, soul, and spirit. Even spiritual presentations made in religious settings are never about making someone feel uncomfortable about his or her beliefs or to prove or disprove the existence of God. Though my aim is to introduce my experience and speak about the dangers of separating ourselves from our loving Creator, all I ask is for my audience to open their hearts and examine the truth that the Creator claims about Himself.

As a former faculty member at the Thomas Jefferson Medical College of Thomas Jefferson University and a member of the curriculum committee at that time, I and my colleagues were charged with the responsibility to change physician/patient approaches to treatment. Instead of a measured scope known as the "biopsychosocial"—a broad view that attributes disease outcome to the intricate, variable interaction of biological factors (genetic, biochemical, etc.), psychological factors (mood, personality, behavior, etc.), and social factors (cultural, familial, socioeconomic)—we were to consider a wider scope known as a "biopsychosocial and spiritual" approach, or the "holistic" approach, to treatment. Since then, the holistic approach has become the standard in every medical school in the US and has been applied throughout the world.

The first national conference on holistic health was held at the University of California, San Diego, School of Medicine in 1975. The American Holistic Health Association (AHHA) and the Holistic

Medical Association were formed soon after. This intriguing new approach was the subject of my presentations in conferences and to the faithful over the years, looking at the total picture of health: physical, emotional, social, intellectual, and spiritual.

The content of this book is targeted not only at educators who will play a part in teaching and empowering youth but most importantly at parents who are responsible for developing their children intellectually, morally, and spiritually. In some Coptic communities (especially those with many new immigrants), I found the congregation tended to steer clear of psychological topics and approaches. They emphasized the spiritual approach to resolving any conflicts they faced in their daily lives. That was perhaps because of their cultural background or lack of knowledge regarding the importance of developing all three spheres of our existence—mind, soul, and spirit. My approach when speaking is to explain there are many good, scientifically based reasons to be open not only to spiritual growth but also personal and emotional development.

On the other hand, one cannot deny that major life stressors can be devastating. The coronavirus pandemic caused a broad range of hardships, including devastating illness and loss of loved ones, failing economy and loss of jobs, marital struggles and divorce, and serious mental illness. Religious beliefs in these challenging times are generally beneficial, helping people cope and deal with most of these problems. Having faith in a higher power and/or believing in God's support facilitates such life transitions. With the support of religious community and clergy, pain and suffering can be reframed into a larger, more benevolent, and passionate concept. Therapeutic relationships now include a variety of spiritually integrated approaches to treatment. These spiritual methods of healing are quite effective and include perseverance, patience, and trusting in a loving, compassionate God. These methods can help people come to terms with resentment, bitterness, and hopelessness. Spirituality also contributes to recognition of our personal and social identity—who we are as Christians and the general meaning of life's purpose and our mission to love, serve, and care for others.

For these reasons, I have addressed the topics in this book via both approaches to spiritual and personal growth. My goal is to contribute to the concept of developing man's mind, soul, and spirit and to further his growth. We can never overlook the fact that spirituality has a unique place in the hearts of the faithful.

Hence, the spiritual presentations made in this text are driven from patristic exegesis, the way Fathers of the Church constructed and interpreted biblical texts. The Church Fathers have been instrumental in helping us understand the scriptures, because they lived in an era and culture closer to the time of the apostles. By relying on the Church Fathers' authentic writings and insightful perspective, I hope to help readers understand their own stances on issues of the day. Most of these spiritual presentations were delivered in Coptic Orthodox Churches, which are grounded in traditional practices dating back to around AD 50. The sources of these traditions are Holy Scripture, liturgical life, the creed and canons of the Ecumenical Councils, the writing of the Church Fathers and lives of saints, and the historical church art.

Presentations that reflect on the development of mind, soul, and spirit may carry with them guiding principles and high but attainable ideals for family life. The focus will be on developing the character and conscience of the children while they still live with the family. The approach to these topics includes how faith formed in children leads to exceptional Christian adults. Professional experience tells us that many problems stem from childhood, and the problems began at home.

Hopefully, this book will inspire families to be well-prepared and to draw courage knowing that God, who gave them those children, also gave them a sacred duty with a promise for a successful mission. That success is based on what He says: "Abide in Me, and I in you. As the branch cannot bear fruit of itself, except it abides in the vine; neither can you, unless you abide in Me" (John 15:4).

O God, You have taught me from my youth;
And to this day I declare Your wondrous works.
Now also when I am old and gray-headed,

ESMAT M. GABRIEL

O God, do not forsake me, Until I declare
your strength to this generation,
Your power to everyone who is to come.)
(Ps. 71:17–18)

BOOK ONE

MEANINGFUL LIVES AND SPIRITUAL JOYS

Living passionately
Rather than feeling purposeless and incredibly frustrated

Chapter One

A WAKE-UP CALL FOR MANKIND

"See, you are very small and frail. A virus that's less than a millionth of your weight was able to bring you down."
—Pope Tawadros II of Alexandria

His Holiness Pope Tawadros II, the 118th and current pope of Alexandria and patriarch of the See of St. Mark, addressing all Coptic Church members in the world regarding the plague of coronavirus pandemic, said,

> When God allows something, remember that He is the Pantocrator; everything is under His control. I see the fact that God has allowed this [coronavirus] pandemic to occur in this form as

an alert to humans to wake up! When a person is asleep, especially when in deep sleep, someone may open a window or remove the cover to wake him up. Out of God's mercy and love, He desires to wake up human beings.

The pope goes on to remind us of how small and weak men and women are, no matter how wealthy or powerful they may be.

God tells us: "See, you are very small and frail. A virus that's less than a millionth of your weight was able to bring you down. Forget about armies, authority, wealth, property, possessions…go back to your real size."
"This is a wakeup call for humankind so that we can reform ourselves," the pope concluded.*

One of his famous quotes long before the coronavirus pandemic would encourage his audience not to fear, and his words are especially relevant today. He said, "Even if humans feel lots of fear, remember God will take care of you. This is a collective message, because fear is contagious… This is a message of reassurance."

---

* Watani International, July 21, 2020.

Chapter Two

LEADER-SERVANT MISSION STATEMENT

Just as the Son of Man did not come to be served, but to serve, and to give His life a ransom for many.
—Matthew 20:28

Purpose

The purpose of the leader-servant mission statement is to build a bonding relationship between colleagues and those whom they serve. A mission statement is essential for clear purpose and enlightenment. The mission for Sunday school, for example, should be to educate, affirm, and inspire new generations and motivate them to want to be part of serving the Lord, not only contributing zealously to serving Him but also extending His kingdom on earth.

A vision statement should be clear and concise, guiding the actions of the Christian servant by spelling out his or her overall goal and providing a path for proper decision-making. It provides the framework or context within which the servant's strategies are formulated.

Mission and vision statements are often confused with one another, and some organizations even use them interchangeably. In simple terms, the mission is the servant's reason for existence, and vision is what he or she wants to accomplish. Every Christian, regardless of his gifts and/or vocation, ought to reveal the Redeemer's character in their lives. Every Christian is called by God to have an influence on the world around us. When Jesus said that we are "the salt of the earth" and "the light of the world," it was not an option; it was a command.

The Mission

The leader-servant's mission is to know, love, and serve God here on earth and be with Him in the hereafter and to get others also to know, love, and serve God here and be with Him in the hereafter.

To Know

The initial step of knowing God is knowledge, but knowing Him is a lifelong experience and is not limited to intellectual activities based on reading, reciting, and even writing or preaching about Him. Knowing God is the soul's search for intimacy with Him. It is longing for Him and needing Him. Realistically, we will never know full intimacy with Him in the fullest measure here on earth. Nevertheless, we need to be cognizant of the fact that knowing God is not a mere collection of information about Him. Intimacy is being connected to God: verbally intimate, emotionally intimate, and spiritually intimate. It means one is in a state of grace and in full communion with Him.

To Love

Loving the Lord means to follow His commandment and to love Him with all your heart, mind, soul, and strength and to love your neighbor as yourself. That's not an easy charge, and we struggle daily to overcome our limitations and failures. In church and prayer, we confess our brokenness and our failures. Many believe that confession and the act of contrition is limited to obvious sins, not knowing that breaking one of these commandments requires repentance and absolution.

4

The measure of perfect love is

- placing God first, neighbor second, and you third;
- being in a state of grace, reconciling to God, to yourself, to your neighbor, and to the creation;
- casting out of all fear; and
- praying for the perfect love of him that indeed casts out all fears.

To Serve

Service is the law of heaven. His angels do always obey. "They serve Him continually" can be said of all who love God. With love there is continuous service in every action, even in rest. We take this not as the end but as the beginning of a new life consecrated to His service—a life of power and joy. St. Irenaeus says,

> To serve God does not mean giving him any gift, nor has God any need of our service. On the contrary, it is he who gives to those who serve him life, immortality and eternal glory. He rewards those who serve him without deriving any benefit himself from their service: he is rich, he is perfect, he has no needs… Consequently, a human being's true glory is to persevere in the service of God.[1]

How can it be done?
St. Thomas Aquinas said the following:

- "Will it"—if there is a will there is a way.
- Obey His will and strive daily to persevere in the religious life.
- Cultivate the humble heart; learn from St. Mary's humility.

According to the Gospel of Luke (1:38), Mary said, "Behold the maidservant of the Lord! Let it be done to me according to your word." In Luke 1:48, Mary said, "My soul magnifies the Lord and my spirit has rejoiced in God my savior. For He has regarded the lowly state of his maidservant." Jesus, who says, "Learn from me, for I am gentle and lowly in heart, and you will find rest for your soul" (Matt. 11:29), desires obedience so that His love and His compassion may have an opportunity to do good for those who serve Him diligently.

Chapter Three

SANCTIFYING CHANGE

In his book *Change We Can Believe In*, President Barrack Obama outlined his vision for change in our country and laid out in detail his plans to fix our economy, make health care affordable for all, achieve energy independence, and keep America secure. How much of this vision has been accomplished will be left to history as it fairly evaluates his legacy.

President-Elect Donald Trump, in his statement on America's future in July 28, 2016, proposed a different vision for America, one that breaks up Washington's rigged system and empowers all Americans to achieve their dreams. His vision was that change is limitless to make America safe and great again. This remains to be seen.

The change that the Lord desires and we ought to seriously pursue in our lives is the sanctification and cleansing of the shameful and corrupt nature of man, which is described throughout the scriptures as an enemy of the spirit. We are introduced to life at natural birth. The new birth—through baptism—is the beginning of spiritual life. The new birth is of God, spiritual, and from above; it does not derive from Abrahamic descent, that is, "of blood" or "of the flesh nor of the will of man."

So to be born of God is to be introduced to real life, to light, to happiness, and to the favor of God. The term expresses at once the greatness and the nature of the change. The question now is, How can we do it?

First, we can do it through a path of emulation by which we acquire virtues that mold us into Christlike beings. The church teaches us that path by learning to trace the footsteps of one of our patron saints then emulating his or her virtues.

Second is the path of guidance. In the book of Proverbs, we read, "Where there is no counsel, the people fall; but the multitude of counselors there is safety" (Prov. 11:14).

The Synaxarium of the Coptic Church declares that one of these great counselors is St. Joseph, the foster father of Jesus. Among the extraordinary titans of faith, among the mystics and popes and abbots and abbesses, among those whose good works have been documented in the annals of history—among all of them, the most powerful saint in heaven besides the Blessed Mother is St. Joseph.

At first glance, you find him shockingly ordinary. But as the Fathers of the Church commented, "It is enough to have the common, simple, and human virtues, but they need to be true and authentic." One needs to examine these virtues and practice each one of them by building into habit a firm disposition to do well. The moral virtues are acquired through human effort aided by God's grace.

Third is to apply the "SMART" rule, which stands for specific, measurable, attainable, realistic/relevant, and time-bound.

Specific examples of St. Joseph's virtues are being just, obedient, silent, enabling, patient, and humble. Notice how all the virtues are derived from the spelling of his name. Measurable—one way to measure is by monitoring our progress daily. Attainable—it is surely attainable by determination and God's grace. Relevant—what is more relevant than to be Christlike, fulfilling His commands to be perfect as our Father in heaven is perfect. Time-bound—instilling a habit takes at least three months to adjust to more positive and virtuous behavior.

It is possible that men can appear to be in nearness to Christ and yet have never learned the reality of His truth, never walked His way nor lived the abandoned life. Most importantly, one may dare to say that many might not even recognize His presence when they meet with Him in confession while He keeps calling, "Come to me, and I will give you rest!" Nor do they truly unite with Him when they partake of his body and blood in Holy Communion. Otherwise, others would see the change engulf their lives and those around them, radiating His light proclaiming His truth.

A second and equally important path to attain change and life transformation is through guidance. Sacred scriptures teach us seek guidance and not to trust in our own strength. St. Dorotheus of Gaza says,

> In fact, we need help: we need guidance and the aid of God. There is nothing more miserable, nothing more risky than people having no one to guide them on the road to God. What does the Scripture say? "Where there is no guidance, a people falls like leaves" ...It is different, however, with those who share their thoughts with others and only act after taking the advice. "In abundance of counselors there is safety." It does not mean by an "abundance of counselors" that one should consult everyone, but that one should always seek advice from those whom one trust most.[2]

Chapter Four

THE THORNY SOIL

The thorny soil represents those who have a complete grasp of the knowledge and the cost of discipleship but are not willing to pay the price. Concern for riches and pleasure outgrow their seeking first the kingdom of God. It is not lack of understanding but lack of commitment, and thus their priorities are reversed. Jesus said, "He, who has ears to hear, let him hear," a wake-up call to each one of us to be vigilant and prepared to clean the soil of thorns. These thorns are the pressure of the secular world and its values. We proclaim that we are in fellowship with Him, yet we find ourselves struggling to bring His fruit to maturity.

It is quite clear to which group we are called to belong. The prophet Jeremiah instructs us to "break up your fallow ground, and sow not among thorns" (Jer. 4:3). So how can we prepare for good ground, hear the word with noble and good heart, and keep it and bear fruit with patience?

First, through *cognitive restructuring* (CR). A number of studies have demonstrated considerable efficacy using this approach therapeutically. It employs many strategies, such as thought recording, i.e., identifying one's disruptive, irrational, or maladaptive thoughts known as "cognitive distortion." Many people tend to magnify problems, overgeneralize issues, and engage in magical thinking that impacts their behavior. In the parable of the sower, there are four types of soil: wayside, rocky ground, soil containing thorns, and good soil. Many believers are under the impression that they are on "good soil," and indeed they may be. But even if it is good soil, the faithful must see to it to increase its fertility so it is further improved and promotes even more healthy, fertile soil.

These processes can occur by enlightening the mind via positive thoughts, for what little inborn light we have can quickly vanish through negligence. Thus, we ought to hold ourselves accountable, striving for simplicity in life and purity in our desires. Such noble methods help us affirm our own belief according to the glorious Gospel of the blessed God, which in turn means that our thoughts are aligned with what we are taught. Our behavior is an expression of who we are—Christlike.

Second, through *thought protraction*, the act of prolonging thought processes that may be hurtful or harmful. To overcome this, the person has to use the ABC method: (A) avoid intrusive thoughts; (B) block disturbing, depressing, and alluring/seductive thoughts; and (C) call on the Lord: "Call to Me, and I will answer you, and show you great and mighty things, which you do not know" (Jer. 33:3).

Third, through *transformation*, the change or renewal from a life that no longer conforms to the ways of the world to one that pleases God (Rom. 12:2). This is accomplished by the renewing of our minds, an inward spiritual transformation that will manifest itself in outward actions. "For indeed, the Kingdom of God is within you" (Luke 17:21). The need then is to turn within to God, asking for grace to help us change and disdain worldly attractions and seeking His consolation and protection.

Fourth, *daily devotions* are important, as they help us spend time with the Lord, which helps us build an intimate relationship with Him. This relationship is formulated while in the presence of the Lord, being exposed to His mercy and divine love. For "Behold, I stand at the door and knock. If anyone hears My voice and open the door, I will come in to him and dine with him, and he with Me" (Rev. 3:20).

11

Chapter Five

HEALING POWERS

It was the faith of the paralytic and of those who carried him that moved Jesus to heal the sick man. Accounts of other miracles reveal more and more Jesus's emphasis on faith as the requisite for exercising His healing powers. In the US Marine Corps, enlisted men live by the Corps' motto "Semper Fidelis," which means "always faithful." A marine is to remain absolutely loyal to his commanders. He pledges his allegiance—even unto death—for the cause of his country. Semper Fidelis would also be an appropriate motto for God's children.

In the case of the paralytic and his four faithful companions, they remained faithful to their mission. As they faced the crowd and saw that there was no hope of forcing a passage, they were determined and empowered by their faith to present a sick man to His healer. It was their task to get the two together somehow, even through the broken roof. As a result, they had succeeded in dropping the patient on his bed right at Christ's feet. Not one of these determined men voiced the words "can't do," for "we cannot" are the coward's words. "We must" are the words of earnest men.

Noteworthy Attributes

Today, we cannot help but be touched by three attributes of the friends of the paralytic besides their faith. It was their confidence, determination, and compassion. Confidence is the feeling or belief that one can rely on someone or something; a firm trust. As an acronym, TRUST stands for "true resolve under severe testing."

Determination is the one indispensable factor in attaining success. In the spiritual path, even more than in material pursuits, our degree of determination makes the crucial difference between fulfilling our spiritual potential and falling short. Compassion means "to suffer together." It is a passionate state of understanding the degree of pain that causes someone to suffer and the feeling that arises and motivates you to care and help even if you don't know the person.

These unique human qualities emanate from being raised in a strong, loving, caring, and trusting environment. In such a safe and secure environment, the child relates well and feels attached to his or her parents. Scientific studies have proven that such a child has a high level of oxytocin in their system and is able to live life with confidence, determination, and the ability to trust and be compassionate toward others and themselves. Oxytocin is a hormone that is made in the brain, in the hypothalamus. It is transported to, and secreted by, the pituitary gland, which is located at the base of the brain. It is released during a crucial time in development and cause the stabilization of the attachment system. Such a stable attachment system encompasses a high level of trust, resulting in feeling secure and compassionate toward self and others. It has been proven that high levels of oxytocin reduce anxiety and fear and counteracts elevated blood pressure and cortisol production associated with stress.

When a child is reared in an environment in which he feels rejected, isolated, and lonely, then he may suffer from a low level of oxytocin. That, in turn, results in an unstable, disturbed attachment system, which will cause a child to experience feelings of distrust, fear, and insecurity. An insecure and untrusting person will find it very hard to get along with others or be capable of finding his place in society, nor will he be able to create a trustworthy relationship with those who care for him.

Finally, the Lord Jesus Christ, physician of our souls and bodies, who forgave the sins of the paralytic and restored him to bodily health, has willed that His church continues through the power of the Holy Spirit and His work of healing and salvation. This is the purpose of the two sacraments of healing: the sacrament of penance and the sacrament of anointing the sick.

Chapter Six

LONELINESS AND EMPTINESS

Loneliness is a strong desire to be connected with others when there is no one or no emotionally satisfying relationship in one's life. Loss of loved ones or friends due to life changes and loss of companionship or social relationship can be devastating. Still, a person can feel lonely no matter whether they have family or friends around.

The feeling of loneliness—though this may sound strange—has a purpose. It triggers the feeling that something important in life is missing. Thus, loneliness motivates the lonely to seek companionship and motivates him or her to take steps to relieve that sense of emptiness.

Emptiness is a human condition that many people suffer from. It is a state of social alienation, apathy, and generalized boredom. Some express it as an "aching emptiness in the heart."

This harsh feeling is often accompanied by sadness, depression, loneliness, and overwhelming despair, says Vivek H. Murthy, the former and current surgeon general of the United States. To combat the opioid epidemic, he launched the "TurnTheTideRx" campaign. Opioids are a class of drug used primarily for pain relief. In one year, opioid overdoses killed more Americans than the entire Vietnam War. During his years of caring for patients, Dr. Murthy said the most common pathology he saw was not heart disease or diabetes but "loneliness."

Loneliness is a growing health epidemic. We live in the most technologically connected age in the history of civilization, yet rates of loneliness have doubled since the 1980s. Loneliness is also associated with a greater risk of cardiovascular disease, dementia, depression, and anxiety, according to Dr. Murthy. Worth than loneliness is emptiness. Loneliness is what you feel when a connection is lost. Emptiness does not come and go in waves; it is static. You don't only feel emptiness, you know it.

Many people think emptiness is due to lack of love, being bored, not being successful in life, or simply not being happy at work. More significantly, emptiness can stem from not being happy in one's marital or family lives. However, none of these situations is a real cause of inner emptiness. Rather than addressing the causes of inner emptiness, people often try to fill the void in their lives with addictive substances such as food, sugar, alcohol, drugs, or nicotine. Another way of trying to fill that vacuum within is through excessive activities, such as watching TV, cruising the internet, working, shopping, spending, gambling, sex, or even bouts of anger and blame.

These approaches may work for some time, but not for long. Soon, the emptiness is back and you are looking for someone or something to temporarily fill the black hole. The problem with all these behaviors is that they only address the symptoms of inner emptiness, not the cause.

How can we overcome this dreadful feeling of loneliness and emptiness? The scriptures today tell us how! Our lives will always be like the fishermen in a boat tossed about on the sea of life, empty and broken (Luke 5:1–11). After a long night of hard work by the sea, the fishermen could not catch any fish. They were bored, empty, idle, and despondent. Even when Jesus came on board and told Simon Peter to put the boat out and cast down his nets, it is the carpenter's son telling a seasoned fisherman how to fish. Simon Peter's response makes it clear that their major effort the night before had totally failed. But here is what he did:

Against his professional judgment, he follows Jesus's command to let down the nets. Simon Peter did not argue or object—he is an example of obedience, humility, and faith. As a result, his life and the lives of fellow fishermen James and John are suddenly changed from idleness to work and from emptiness to fullness as they catch huge loads of fish and their boats start sinking from the weight.

But that's only the beginning of treating the symptoms of emptiness, idleness, and boredom. Treating the inner emptiness is seen at the point when Simon Peter realized that he was in the overwhelming presence of the Lord and a surging feeling exposed him to give account of himself to God. So he fell down at Jesus's knees, saying, "Depart from me, for I am a sinful man, O' Lord!" Inner healing followed, and the reward came when Jesus said to Simon Peter, "Do not be afraid. From now on you will catch men." For the Lord does not call the qualified, but He qualifies whom he calls. The Lord needs confession of our sins and repentance, and that's exactly what Simon Peter did.

However, the healing of inner emptiness is not complete until we learn to forsake all our earthly care for possessions, worldly matters, and distractions. That is exactly what the disciples did—they forsook all and followed Him.

Chapter Seven

SOURCE OF JOY

The online encyclopedia Theopedia describes joy as "a state of mind and an orientation of the heart. It is a settled state of contentment, confidence, and hope." The ultimate source of this state of mind is the most joyful event in all of human history—the Incarnation, or when God became man and dwelt among us.

When Christ's birth was announced to Mary, she certainly had plans for her life before the Annunciation. She had become betrothed and surely looked forward to a normal life within her community, raising a family and perhaps finding some ease of life. Mary put all of that aside in a moment when the Lord made His will known to her and put her trust totally in Him. Mary said, "Behold the maidservant of the Lord. Let it be done to me according to your word" (Luke 1:38).

We have the gift of free will, which means we have our own ideas about how our lives are to go. That is our gift from God and the manner in which we are made in His image. However, if we want to live joyfully, we, too, are to follow the example of Mary's fiat and make ourselves into willing and joyful disciples of Jesus, with complete trust in the Lord as to His will. St. Mary not only lights the way with her fiat, her humility, and her faith but also with her praise of the Lord: "My soul magnifies the Lord and my spirit has rejoiced in God my Savior…For He who is mighty has done great things for me, and holy is His name" (Luke 1:47, 49).

Joyous Behaviors

Intimacy: Like St. Mary, we must always desire to seek and spend devotional time with Him. The psalmist declares, "Let the hearts of those who seek the Lord rejoice" (Ps. 105:3). St. Augustine said our heart is restless until it rests in God. St. Mary's joyous attitude, stable disposition, and years spent in the temple merited God's favor and blessed her by His Grace.

Equanimity: This refers to mental calmness, composure, and evenness of temper, especially in a difficult situation. St. Mary was in a state of serenity and calmness that allowed her to meditate, concentrate, and consider what the angel said and what manner of greeting this was!

Aspiration: A life of aspiration illuminates us and liberates us. There is a deep and profound strength accepting angel Gabriel's proclamation that "the Holy Spirit will come upon you, and the power of the Highest will overshadow you." It is important that we believe this promise encompasses all God's baptized children as well as His sanctifying grace when we partake of the Holy Communion and transform into what we consume.

Self-mastery (temperance): This is the ability to let go of ownership and ego and to defer or do without gratification. It is the willpower to overcome passions and indulgence and to enjoy the good things in life in moderation. St. Mary's well-developed human virtues governed her reaction at the Annunciation to the great news that the Holy One who was to be born would be called the Son of God; she responded with extreme humility, "Behold the maidservant of the Lord!" Also, when St. Elizabeth greeted her, saying, "Blessed are you among women and blessed the fruit of your womb! But why is this granted to me, that the mother of my Lord come to me?" St. Mary again praised the Lord in all humility. "He has regarded the lowly state of His maidservant." What is this unsurpassed degree of humility from the one who perfectly embodies the obedience of faith?

Chapter Eight

OVERCOMING REJECTION

Our Lord Jesus was sent by the Father to bring God's salvation to the world. He was anointed by the Father to preach the Gospel, heal the brokenhearted, give sight to the blind, provide deliverance to those in captivity, and liberate the oppressed. Initially, listeners in the synagogue were impressed by Jesus's preaching, but they took offense when He mentioned God's miracles that favored both the widow of Sidon and the cleansing of Naaman the Syrian. His preaching of these stories signaled that God had chosen the Gentiles over the Jews to perform His miracles and extend His grace. Their offense soon turned into rage and rejection, for they did not want to submit to His teaching and His lordship. They rose up against Him, chased Him out of the city, and wanted to throw Him over a cliff (Luke 4:14–30).

That was then. Nowadays, rejection is rampant in the domestic church, in Christian homes, and among our own families. Rejection is defined as "the attitudes and actions of others that signal to us that we are not worthy, but are worthless." Rejection creates surges of anger and aggression. The people in the synagogue, once afflicted with feelings of rejection, became enraged and wanted to kill the preacher of the good news.

In 2001, the US surgeon general issued a report stating that rejection was a greater risk for causing adolescent violence than drugs, poverty, or gang membership. A feeling of rejection is expressed in many forms, including anger, aggression, name-calling, insults, condescension, indifference, self-centeredness, and silence. These are just some of the unhealthy behaviors that can develop in our daily life, either in our homes or outside.

Today is the beginning of the Coptic New Year, and the virtuous goal one can strive for is to get rid of any unhealthy behaviors. Each member of our families should be cognizant of these destructive attitudes and actions toward a spouse or a child that signal to them that they are rejected, not worthy, or are worthless.

On this blessed day, we need to examine our behavior and eliminate any trace of unwanted or unacceptable behavior that could dampen positive feelings in those around us. The effect of such negative behavior is displayed in many forms, ranging from poor self-esteem, hopelessness, sadness, and depression to anxiety and phobias. This may also lead a person to a state of isolation, loneliness, and self-destruction.

The opposite of rejection is the amplified desire for acceptance that keeps many people from developing a well-balanced and wholesome personality. They tend to mimic others' behaviors in order to gain and retain acceptance and a sense of belonging at any cost. Yet the person who operates out of a fear of rejection all too often ends up pushing away members of their own family and friends who care about them the most. When loved ones pull away, it appears to be rejection, and the vicious cycle continues as we reject others just as we have been rejected.

The basis for these behaviors is our cynical view of previous experiences. Cynicism about relationships is a huge handicap—it will stop us from every divine plan God makes for us. The solution is to restore and harmonize our relationships within our families, sooner rather than later. We should trust in the Lord for the remedy from cynical reluctance so that we may positively relate to others. We should treat all family members with justice and fairness: "Say to the just all is well" (Isa. 3:10). Yes, all is well when we seek only the divine will.

Chapter Nine

PRICELESS TREASURE OF TRUST

During the journey of life, we often find out that the prodigal son is a reality of many if not most of our families today. The prodigal son in the Scriptures is the story of a rebellious son who rejects his father's upbringing. As Christian parents, we soon realize that regardless of how hard we strive to raise our children, there are no guarantees they will turn out as we may have hoped…loving and trusting the Lord. No matter how hard we teach our children about God and His word, and no matter how often we pray for our children and encourage them to go to church, some decide to walk away from all that we taught them. Hopefully they will come to their senses and return someday as the prodigal son did.

Even in those families where God is loved, trusted, and glorified, children sometimes rebel and run from their roots for good! St. Paul pointed this out when he said of his "fellow worker" Demas: "He has forsaken me, having loved this present world." Demas was trusted and honored, a man of some maturity and advancement, and he was now guilty of the base act of leaving the apostle (2 Tim. 4:10).

In the prodigal son story, the son returns home, repentant and willing to do anything to be among his father's household even as a hired servant. What made him say now, "I will rise and go to my father"? The answer is he must have trusted his father. He knew deep in his heart that nothing could get in the way of his father's kindness, patience, and unconditional love. After all, his father was the one who did not object to his son's rebellious act and willingly gave him his share of the inheritance.

The key word here is "trust." Trust is the cornerstone of effective interpersonal relationships. I once learned and admired what the acronym for the word "trust" stands for, and it says it all:

T: Turn to the Lord and lay your burden at His feet. Remember His promise: "Ask, and it will be given to you; seek, and you will find; knock, and it will be opened to you" (Matt. 7:7). Also let us remember to dial the Lord's "333" hotline: "Call to Me, and I will answer you, and show you great and mighty things, which you do not know" (Jer. 33:3).

R: Realize that coming to earth is part of our Heavenly Father's plan to restore our physical body in His image, give us an example to follow in His steps (1 Peter 2:21), and learn from Him, for he is "gentle and humble in heart" (Matt. 11:29). So let's remember that He has a plan for our lives that may not be according to what we want or wish for but rather for His will be done on earth as it is in heaven.

U: Understand that you do not understand, "For My thoughts are not your thoughts, nor are your ways My ways," says the Lord (Isa. 55:8).

S: Seek God always. "Seek first the kingdom of God and His righteousness, and all these things shall be added to you" (Matt. 6:33).

T: Thank God always. "Give thanks to the Lord for he is good! For His mercy endures forever" (Ps. 118:29).

Chapter Ten

DEALING WITH ANXIETY AND FEAR

Spiritual and Psychological Implications

"Therefore, do not worry saying, 'What shall we eat?' or 'What shall we drink?' or 'What shall we wear?'" (Matt. 6:31).

Very reverently, I would like to talk about a subject we hear about every day and seems to have a grip over our lives. In scripture, the Lord says "not to worry," yet it appears that we worry all the time. We live in an age marked by high anxiety and fear.

While there is a difference between worry and anxiety, worry tends to affect the mind, whereas anxiety affects both mind and body. Anxiety is a psychological and physiological state characterized by somatic, emotional, cognitive, and behavioral components. It is the displeasing feeling of concern, characterized by increased levels of fear, worry, uneasiness, and dread. Such feelings are usually considered normal reactions to pressure or stress. They may help an individual deal with a demanding situation by prompting them to cope with it. When anxiety becomes excessive, however, it may fall under the classification of an anxiety disorder.

It is advisable, though, that we differentiate between anxiety and fear. Anxiety is a generalized mood that can occur without an identifiable triggering stimulus. As such, it is distinguished from fear, which is an appropriate cognitive and emotional response to a perceived threat (e.g., one who is concerned about his health or the health of a loved one will experience concern or fear). Additionally, fear is related to the specific behaviors of escape and avoidance, whereas anxiety is related to situations perceived as uncontrollable or unavoidable.

Overcoming Fear

How can we find release when we are gripped with fear? King David told us. During a perilous time in his life, he wrote, "I sought the Lord, and he heard me, and delivered me from all my fears... The angel of the Lord encamps all around those who fear Him, and deliver them" (Ps. 34:4, 7). In dark and difficult days, David experienced the security of God's presence and the light of His Love. That's why he could say, "Oh, taste and see that the Lord is good; blessed is the man who trusts in Him!"

According to St. John Climacus, also known as John of the Ladder (a sixth- to seventh-century monk at the monastery on Mount Sinai), "Fear is really a lack of faith that becomes obvious when we think of what unforeseen things might happen. It is lack of trust in God. Fear in his view steams from the proud soul. Such a soul is a slave to fear precisely because it trusts in itself rather than God. Thus, it lacks humility and being full of pride shudders at any noise or any shadow."[3]

As we clinically differentiate fear/concern from other mood disorders, so does St. John Climacus. Bodily fear may help an individual deal with a demanding situation by prompting him to cope with it. St. John also states, "Sometimes only the body is afraid and the fear has not spread to the soul, then you are nearly cured."[4] Excessive worry and fear ought to be fought as one would fight a plague. Fear, even the smallest fear, hacks at the cords of love that bind the faithful creature to his Creator. In clinical practice, professionals treat fear and anxiety as a possible cause to despondency or depression. They define the condition as "apprehension, tension, or uneasiness that stems from the anticipation of danger, which may be internal or external. Although anxiety and fear are distinguishable, the symptoms are similar and fall into four main groups: motor tension, automatic hyperactivity, anxious rumination, and vigilance and scanning.[5]

To treat these symptoms, clinicians usually use cognitive behavioral therapy. This is a combination of cognitive therapy, which can modify or eliminate thought patterns contributing to the patient's symptoms, and behavioral therapy, which aims to help the patient change his or her behavior.

Biblical Approach

The clinician usually conducts a careful search for the thoughts, feelings, and causes of these variables. The goal is to identify major life conflicts, develop behavioral and cognitive strategies, and increase understanding of beliefs and messages that reduce worry and anxiety.

In the Gospel, the master of the soul and supreme counselor addresses these very issues and tells us how to overcome our anxieties. He who knows major life conflicts needs to only "lay up treasures in heaven," where one doesn't have to worry and develop fear from destructive "moth nor rust." Neither will we be worried about thieves breaking in and stealing from us (Matt. 6:19–20).

The heart of discipleship lies in disentangling ourselves (behavioral approach) from the chains of earthly things and attaching ourselves to God, the true treasure. Later, we will focus on behavioral themes and conduct that help us become attached to Him. These specific steps will also help us to lay up for ourselves treasures in heaven. The Lord also asks us to recognize entry sources (e.g., eyes) and to develop behavioral and cognitive strategies.

Jesus points out that "the lamp of the body is the eye." The mind (cognition) is the spiritual eye of the soul; it illuminates the inner man and governs the will. Keeping the mind wholesome and pure is fundamental to the Christian life. Then the Lord speaks of life's mission and who truly has control over it. An earthly master will always subject us to tyranny of his demands and force us to worry and become fearful of what might happen to us should we falter.

The Lord warns us that the cause of our anxieties and fears is in trying to serve two masters. People attempt to maintain an attachment to both earthly and heavenly things. But this is impossible, since both demand full allegiance. The Lord calls mammon ("riches") a master not because wealth is evil by nature but because of the control it has over people.

A "cognitive restructuring" is a prerequisite to increasing understanding of beliefs and messages. An appropriate change of behavior should follow as well to negate obsession with earthly matters and eliminate the worry and anxiety we otherwise suffer. All these are beneficial and therapeutic approaches, though they are more than that: they are divine providence to help God's children lead a peaceful life. Whoever has ears, let him hear!

Steps for Laying Up Heavenly Treasures

To maintain a tranquil heart and peaceful mind, one has to rise above merely external worship that does not avail with God. It must be joined with internal sincerity and appropriate conduct in our daily life. Fasting and other ascetic acts do not necessarily indicate virtue. St. Augustine reminds us that even heretics fast! God will not see these actions if we mistreat others. In Isaiah 58:6–8, the Lord speaks of a chosen fast that pleases Him:

- To loosen the bonds of wickedness
- To undo heavy burdens
- To let the oppressed go free
- To break every yoke
- To share your bread with the hungry
- To bring to your house the poor who are cast out
- To cover the naked when you see him
- And not hide yourself from your own flesh

"Then your light shall break forth like the morning, your healing shall spring forth speedily, and your righteousness shall go before you; the glory of the Lord shall be your rear guard. Then you shall call, and the Lord will answer; You shall cry and He will say, 'Here I am'" (Isa. 58:9).

Chapter Eleven

LISTENING ATTENTIVELY!

If you then, being evil, know how to give good gifts
to your children, how much more will your Father in
heaven give the Holy Spirit to those who ask Him!
—Luke 11:13

Many years ago, an annoyed seventy-six-year-old man from Richmond Heights, a suburb of Saint Louis, received a call from the White House. President Ronald Reagan was trying to call, yet the man hung up on him more than six times. Mr. Robert German, who sold caps and hats from his home, said, "I thought he was crazy, so I hung up," convinced that the caller was a crank. When "the operator insisted it was Washington, DC," and announced that the call was from the White House, he did not believe the operator and thought it was a hoax. It took the Bell Telephone Company, assisted by a neighbor, to finally convince Mr. German it was for real. As a result, the man has the privilege of chatting with President Reagan for about fifteen minutes.[6]

This incident reminds us of a call received centuries ago by a young Israelite named Samuel (1 Sam. 3:1–10). He did not realize who was calling despite it being repeated. The caller this time was greater than a president. Only when Eli told him to respond and say, "Speak LORD for Your servant hears" did he listen.

What about us? God calls each one of us today and speaks every day through His written Word, the Bible (2 Tim. 3:16–17). But no one can comprehend the thoughts of God except the Spirit of God

(1 Cor 2:11), who reveals God's word, made known to us through Christ. The Spirit, who "has spoken through the prophets," makes us hear the Father's word and understand it, for we cannot gain it on our own. Before we even begin to study, we ought to tune ourselves to the Spirit within and ask Him to guide us. The Spirit of truth who unveils Christ to us "will not speak on his own" (John 16:13). That is why the world cannot understand the word on its own. For "the world cannot receive, because it neither sees him nor knows him," while those who believe know the Spirit because He dwells with them and will be in them (John 14:17).

Thus, we need to approach the Bible with a humble attitude and set a time for setting daily in the presence of the Lord as Mary did, attentively listening to him. Despite the overwhelming task of preparing a meal for Christ and other house guests that Martha had to deal with, Mary was detached from her sister's demands to help prepare the meal. The Lord commended Mary, for she chose what was better, and it would not be taken away from her, for Mary listened while Martha labored.

The important questions are these: Do we hear Him? Do we take the time daily to listen to Him? And do we ask Him for the much better gift of all—the Holy Spirit? St. Augustine struggled to change his life because he did not completely understand who God was, nor did he understand the emptiness he felt in prayers when he was young. After he finally converted to Christianity, he reflected on his enlightened spirit, writing in his book *Confessions*:

> Late have I loved you, O Beauty ever ancient, ever new, late have I loved you! You were within me, but I was outside, and it was there that I searched for you. In my unloveliness I plunged into the lovely things which you created. You were with me, but I was not with you. Created things kept me from you; yet if they have not been in you, they would have not been at all. You called, you shouted and broke through my deafness; You flashed, you shone, and you dis-

pelled my blindness. You breathed your fragrance on me; I gasped, and now I pant for you; I have tested you, now I hunger and thirst for more; You, touched me, and I burned for your peace.

Chapter Twelve

CHRISTIAN VIEWS ON SUBSTANCE USE

Just as Jesus healed the blind and mute man over two thousand years ago, today members of the body of Christ ought to be earnestly working and praying for a multitude of blind and mute people who are possessed by the demon of addiction. On October 26, 2017, President Donald Trump declared a nationwide public health emergency to combat the opioid crisis. He called it "the worst drug crisis in American history." The president said 64,000 Americans died from overdoses in a single year—175 every day, 7 every hour. Then the president sadly spoke about his brother's death due to alcoholism.

Parents should know that research shows that the main reason children do not use drugs, alcohol, or tobacco is because of their parents' positive influence and because they know it would disappoint them. Teaching children to absolutely fear taking drugs, other than medically with permission of a parent, is a must. This lesson needs to start as young as five or six years old. Keep it simple for young kids, but be serious. Bend down and look into their eyes, showing them you mean business. You might say, "Never, ever take a pill or any medicine from any one, not even a friend, no matter what they tell you. You can become addicted!" As they get older, you can discuss the dangers of addiction in greater depth.

The Root Cause

The root cause of this devastating problem is that many families live in a divided household. A divided family unit, abuse, and trauma are sources of family problems. Abusive or traumatic relationship is most likely to cause a spouse or child to experience an overwhelming emotional threat to his or her life. Though such conditions may or may not lead to addiction, research clearly indicates a connection between addiction and traumatic experience. That is why the Lord says every house divided will not stand, yet one dares to say that divided homes have grown significantly in the Christian community due to the impact of technology on all members of the family but especially the children.

Most family members nowadays are constantly involved in the digital world, from texting and playing games to downloading music and surfing their favorite websites. These activities by their very nature limit a child's availability to communicate with their parents and siblings. Both popular culture and technology have contributed to a growing divide between the traditional roles that children and their parents play. Over the past two decades, children who watch reality shows and other television programming have received messages from popular culture telling them that parents are selfish, immature, or even incompetent. As "digital natives" (i.e., having always had computers and the internet in their lives), children found an unprecedented degree of independence from parental supervision and guidance. Thus, they are under the impression they have gained a sense of superiority over their parents, who still struggle with the new technology.

Surprisingly enough, in an attempt to counteract this growing divide, parents began communicating with their children in cyberspace rather than with actual face-to-face interaction. So it's not only the children who are responsible for the growing divide—parents can be equally responsible for contributing to it. Most likely they are too busy working or living in their own technological world, such as talking on their mobile phones, using their iPad, or watching TV when they could be sharing activities or generally connecting with their children. The ramifications of this distancing are profound; it causes poor communication skills and ultimately poor family relationships.

As a result, children are less able to model healthy behavior, share positive values, and live together in harmony. This could be a cause for children to feel insecure, alienated, and distant and could easily expose them to risky influences online. It is the parent's responsibility to get their house in order and to set their children as their priority. It starts by structuring the time when they use or access their own digital world. Thus, they could teach their children to emulate their own appropriate use of technology, showing them how to put down their devices when it's time for family to sit around the dinner table or spend leisure time together.

Faith: A Source of Health and Healing

Love and harmonious relations between spouses and children are essential. This is hugely important to create a mutually respectful and enriching family dynamic that involves clear, heartfelt communication, understanding, and acceptance. The core of this unique relationship is based on the rock of family prayers and an active spiritual life. Both are keys for a drug-free family life. The family that prays together stays together without losing a loved one to drugs. Such an active spiritual life will not be complete, however, without being part of the church communal life.

"Woe to him who is alone when he falls, for he has no one to help him up" (Eccles. 4:10). Prayer in the community church is the most intense expression of our faith in God and commitment to His purpose in the world. Partaking of the Holy Communion unites us with Christ and with one another in His sacramental body and blood. As members of His body, we are called by the Holy Spirit to continue Christ's saving work of reconciliation and by His grace help to extend His kingdom on earth.

Chapter Thirteen

THE EXCELLENCE OF MAN

Aiden Wilson Tozer, a well-known, well-published American Christian Pastor and author, once described character as "the excellence of moral beings." As the excellence of gold is its purity and the excellence of art is its beauty, so the excellence of man is his character. Godly character is the result of the Holy Spirit's work of sanctification. It is the purity of heart that God gives becoming purity in action.

How can we then strive for purity of heart? Jesus gives us the answer: we can look at the "fruit" in our lives. Faith-filled hearts will produce much spiritual fruit. According to the epistle to the Galatians, the fruit of the Holy Spirit includes: "love, joy, peace, patience, kindness, goodness, faithfulness, gentleness, and self-control." Another fruit is to do what we can to share God's truth with others. Now the question is why these wonderful virtues and attributes may not be apparent in some of us as believers.

The answer is, good soil is free of rocks and weeds. So our hearts and minds should also be free of the bad seeds by which the world tries to inflict significant damage to our spiritual life. Regretfully, there are three kinds of "heart soil" that don't bear any kind of spiritual fruit. One is when people don't share with others the truth that is deep down in their hearts; instead they meet to gossip and spread rumors, and their hearts grow dull. For others, their lives are overly busy with the cares of this world full of worry, fear, and frustration. And thirdly, it's when others think more about themselves, building their own empire rather than serving the Lord and extending His kingdom on earth.

If this sounds like your life, there is only one way to make a change! Jesus says He is the *way* (John 14:6). Confess. Tell the Lord that your heart has not been good soil. Ask Him to replace the hardness of your heart with a good, soft heart that will be the perfect place for His truth to take root and grow. Listen to God's promise: "I will give you a new heart and put a new spirit within you. I will take the heart of stone out of your flesh and give you a heart of flesh" (Ezek. 36:26).

As children of God who care about extending His kingdom, we also can see ourselves the sower in this story. Be prepared as you begin to share the good news about Jesus with others; some will accept and some will decline. You are asked only to spread the seed, for each person has the free will whether to accept the truth. It is always right, though, to pray for God to soften the hearts of those you speak to!

Finally, character is influenced and developed by our free will and choices. Daniel "resolved not to defile himself" in Babylon (Dan. 1:8), and that godly choice was an important step in formulating an unassailable integrity in the young man's life. Character, in turn, influences our choices. "The integrity of the upright will guide them" (Prov. 11:3). Character will help us weather the storms of life and keep us from sin (Prov. 10:9).

Recently I read of a young man of Christian character named DeVon Franklin who is a Hollywood producer and bestselling author. He authored a book titled *The Hollywood Commandments: A Spiritual Guide to Secular Success*. He is also an award-winning maker of Christian films and TV shows merging his passion and his faith. While he was at Sony, he helped make a series of hit faith films: *Heaven Is for Real* and *Miracles from Heaven*. His latest projects include an animated retelling of the Nativity called *The Star*. He believes he was called to change the agnostic secular world of Hollywood and says, "If you are being called to an industry, it is how you navigate that industry, not how you allow the industry to navigate you." Most importantly, he sees himself as the salt and light that preserve the world from the evil inherent in a society of ungodly men whose unredeemed natures are corrupted by sin (Ps. 14:3).

Chapter Fourteen

THE COST OF A FREE OFFER!

Early in my career, I worked at Philadelphia State Hospital, a psychiatric hospital, where I met a colleague who was a private pilot. He owned a "BJ" or business jet and loved to fly. He knew how much passion I had for flying, so he invited me to come along for a free ride in his airplane. My superior convinced me to decline his offer, because my friend was still a beginner and in accepting his offer, I would have committed my very life to him. If he flies safely, I am safe; if he crashes, I die—it's as simple as that. In other words, the instant I say yes to his free offer, I am totally committed to him. I have entrusted my very life into his hands.

Far different but similarly, the Lord Jesus freely offers His salvation to everyone who accepts and believes. But we need to understand that when we receive His free offer, we are no longer our own; we have been bought with a price. Thus, to truly follow Christ, we must consider the cost of discipleship. He warns us not to begin to follow Him superficially, only to turn back later when things get tough. Luke 14:25 says, "Great multitudes went with Him," so He turned to them and laid out the demands of discipleship.

Making the decision to follow Him entails careful, detailed, rational thinking, not an impulsive decision made in the heat of the moment without much thought about the consequences. One needs to "sit down first and count the cost," referring to the man building the tower (Luke 14:28), and "sit down and take counsel," referring to the king considering going to war (Luke 14:31). Here are the three costs that He spells out:

First, we must hate our families and ourselves (Luke 14:26). The Lord means that our allegiance and love for Him must be so great that by comparison, our love for our families and even for our own lives looks like hatred. Normally, there is no conflict between loving Christ and our family members also. But sometimes a tug of war develops among members of the family because of our belief and faith and their disbelief and their demand to abandon our love for Christ.

Second, we must carry our own cross (Luke 14:27). The Lord Jesus here is looking at the process of daily death of the ego and selfish desires and of the willingness to bear reproach for His name's sake. So why was Jesus prompting cross-bearing? Because He wanted disciples who were willing to face the difficulties it would take to serve His cause.

Third, we must forsake all that we have (Luke 14:33). Jesus is pointing at the fact that there are two possible lords we can serve, and the two are exclusive: God or mammon (material wealth). Most of us think that we can combine them, with God taking the lead. But Jesus says that won't work: "You cannot serve God and mammon" (Matt. 6:24). He continues in the Gospel of Luke, "No servant can serve two masters; for either he will hate the one and love the other, or else he will be loyal to one and despise the other" (Luke 16:13).

No doubt Jesus's words here are tough and sobering! We all fall short, but we must honestly work to follow His commands, applying them to our hearts. These worthwhile costs are still our challenge today. Are we willing to take the cross and serve Christ in self-denial? To follow Christ truly, we must put Him above everything else in life. He alone deserves to be first above everything else in all of our lives, because He is the Lord God who willingly offered Himself on the cross for our sins!

The task is great, but it is extremely important and eternally rewarding. Fear not, for His love is great and His grace will suffice and help us reach our destiny.

Chapter Fifteen

GOD'S AMAZING POWER

"Rejoice, highly favored one, the Lord is with you; blessed are you among women!"

—Luke 1:28

Rejoice!

For those who are anxious, despondent, and agonizing about living and life, the word today is "rejoice," the Gospel of good news is here! The first words of angel Gabriel to Mary were, "Rejoice, highly favored one, the Lord is with you; blessed are you among women!" Such heavenly joy that gladdens the heart is quite a gift to receive. On the contrary, the world's joy is fleeting and empty. St. Augustine said, "The world's joy is vanity. We long for it to come, but when it has come, we fail to hold on to it."[7]

Fear Not!

To those who fear the future and what it could bring, the word today is, "Do not be afraid, Mary, for you have found favor with God." Fear is one of the evil's most potent forces. Believers must fight fear as they would fight a plague. Perfect love casts out fear, and the only way to obtain this perfect love, to dispel fear, is to love Jesus more and more in our lives. We can only banish fear by being mindful of the Lord's presence in our lives and calling on His Name all the time…Jesus, help me. Jesus, provide. Jesus, heal me.

Who Jesus Is!

To those who use God's name in vain, the proclamation of who Jesus is has to be one of the most exalted in all scripture: "He will be great, and will be called the Son of the Highest; and the Lord God will give Him the throne of His father David. And He will reign over the house of Jacob forever, and of His kingdom there will be no end" (Luke 1:32–33).

The Triune God

To those who do not understand our triune God, the Trinity is an unfathomable and yet unmistakable doctrine in scripture. The wonderful exchange between Mary and the angel Gabriel continues to express God's pure and simple gift to Mary: "The Holy Spirit will come upon you, and the power of the Most High will overshadow you; therefore, also, that Holy One who is to be born will be called Son of God" (Luke 1:35). Within this single verse, we have the basis for why the Christian faith is centered in the triune God. All three persons are present in the God we confess as the highest, in Jesus Christ as the Son of God, and in the overshadowing presence of the Holy Spirit.

Faith

To those who doubt or lack faith, let's learn from Mary's final response, which expresses her faith as the young mother and chosen one of God: "Behold the maidservant of the Lord! Let it be to me according to your word" (Luke 1:38).

The Impossible Made Possible!

To those who cannot believe that God can make the impossible possible, let's think deeply about Elizabeth, Mary's relative, who had conceived a son in her old age despite being considered barren. "For with God nothing will be impossible" (Luke 1:37).

Chapter Sixteen

THE POWER OF PRAYER

The eyes of the Lord are on the righteous and
His ears are open to their prayers.

—1 Peter 3:12

There is certainly great power in private and public prayers, especially in Holy Liturgy and sacraments by which Christ divine life is
made available to the faithful. Christ also taught that wherever two
or three are gathered together in His name, "I am there in midst of
them" (Matt. 18:20).

The Lord speaks of private prayers and how we should go to our
rooms, close our doors, and pray to our Father who sees us in secret
and will reward us openly (Matt. 6:6). He urged us to pray to flee
from temptation and stay strong in the face of trials and never to lose
heart (Mark 13:35, Luke 18:1, Luke 21:36). He also taught us the
Our Father to know both how to pray and what we ought to pray for.
On the Lord's Prayer, St. Gregory of Nyssa said,

> Anyone with a bit of good sense would not make
> so bold as to call God by the name of the Father
> until he had come to be like him… So if one
> of us, in examining himself, discovers that his
> conscience is covered in mud and needs to be
> cleansed, he cannot allow himself such familiar-
> ity with God. First, he must be purified. Then
> why, in this prayer of his, does the Lord Jesus

teach us to call God by the name of Father? I suppose that, in suggesting this word, he is only putting before our eyes the holiest life as the criterion of our behavior.[8]

Unanswered Prayers!

In an alienated marriage, prayers are not answered. The apostle Peter warns married people, "Likewise you husbands, dwell with them with understanding, giving honor to the wife, as to the weaker vessel, and as being heirs together of the grace of life, that your prayers may not be hindered" (1 Peter 3:7). However, the prayers of even a righteous couple might not be answered. Both Zacharias and Elizabeth probably prayed passionately for years for a son but eventually gave up. Advanced in years, they naturally stopped believing they would ever have a child. Then an angel of the Lord appeared to Zacharias, standing on the right side of the altar of incense. Zacharias was troubled, and fear fell upon him.

> The angel said to him, "Do not be afraid, Zacharias, for your prayer is heard; and your wife Elizabeth will bear you a son, and you shall call his name John. And you will have joy and gladness, and many will rejoice at his birth. For he will be great in the sight of the Lord, and shall drink neither wine nor strong drink. He will also be filled with the Holy Spirit, even from his mother's womb." (Luke 1:13–15)

When Zacharias heard the announcement, he may have thought, "I don't know what you are talking about. I no longer pray for a son, for both my wife and I are old. I gave up on that prayer a long time ago. I am praying for the salvation of Israel. I'm praying that God will send the promised Messiah."

Zacharias didn't know that God would answer both prayers at once and use his miracle baby to be Christ's forerunner to prepare the way for Him. Later, the Lord would give witness to John's importance: "Assuredly I say to you, among those born of women there has not risen one greater than John the Baptist" (Matt. 11:11).

Zacharias had probably completely given up on the idea of being a father; it was a hope that was crushed over the years of disappointment. But God hadn't given up on it, even though Zacharias and Elizabeth had.

When we are in that place, we sometimes begin to doubt God's love and care for us. But God always loves, and His care never stops. For "the eyes of the Lord are on the righteous and His ears are open to their prayers" (1 Peter 3:12). It has been said that there are qualifiers; God answers prayers in one of three ways: (1) yes, (2) no, or (3) wait.

Chapter Seventeen

GIGANTIC WOMEN!

When the feminist movement of the 1960 and '70s began, it was to fight for the belief that men and women should have equal rights and opportunities. Needless to say, this is what the Creator has intended from the beginning, for He created man and woman equal. Yet the issue of equality remains alive and well. When I have spoken in Christian communities, I have often been asked the question: Why shouldn't a woman be a priest? Or in our Coptic churches the question is: Why can't girls be ordained as deacons?

The answer to that stems from scripture. We find women not only equal but held in high regard as well. St. Luke, in the first chapter of his Gospel, directs the spotlight toward two godly women. They are Elizabeth, the soon-to-be mother of John the Baptist, and Mary, the mother-to-be of the Messiah. Both were truly great and godly women. Both were humble women of no social or economic standing. Yet the worship of both of these women is such that they are models for all true disciples of our Lord and hopefully are models for all women of this world.

In such prominence and high regard, we find the angel addressing Mary: "Rejoice, highly favored one, the Lord is with you, blessed are you among women" (Luke 1:28)! Witnessing this glorious scene and hearing these marvelous greeting, Mary was somewhat troubled, but the angel said to her,

> Do not be afraid, Mary, for you have found favor
> with God. And behold, you will conceive in your

womb and bring forth a Son and shall call His
name Jesus. He will be great, and will be called
the Son of Most High, and the Lord will give
him the throne of his ancestor David. He will
reign over the house of Jacob forever, and of His
kingdom there will be no end. (Luke 1:30–33)

Slightly perplexed, Mary said to the angel, "How can this be,
since I do not know a man?" The angel answered, "The Holy Spirit
will come upon you, and the power of the Highest will overshadow
you; therefore, also, that Holy One is to be born will be called the Son
of God" (Luke 1:34–35). In humility of faith, Mary said, "Behold the
maidservant of the Lord. Let it be done to me according to your word"
(Luke 1:38). This is one great woman indeed, Mary "the Magnificat."

Before departing, the angel told Mary about the other great woman
when he said to her, "Now indeed, Elizabeth your relative has also conceived a son in her old age; and this is now her six month for her who was
called barren. For with God nothing will be impossible" (Luke 1:36–
37). Mary then arose and went hastily to visit Elizabeth. Both Elizabeth
and her husband, Zacharias, were "righteous before God, walking in all
His commandments and ordinances of the Lord blameless" (Luke 1:6).
They also were promised a son who would be "great in the sight of the
Lord, and shall drink neither wine nor strong drink. He will also be filled
with the Holy Spirit, even from his mother's womb" (Luke 1:15). What
a family and what a great woman and a mother she is!

When Elizabeth heard Mary's greetings upon her arrival, she
was filled with the Holy Spirit and spoke with a loud voice, "Blessed
are you among women and blessed is the fruit of your womb! But
why is this granted to me, that the mother of my Lord should come
to me" (Luke 1:41–43)? These were two gigantic women full of
grace by whom and through whom salvation of the human race was
accomplished. Emulating their model of humility, faith, hope, and
love will elevate any woman to be a holy and prominent individual.
And regardless of which role a woman occupies within the structure
of the church, a holy and prominent woman will remain an honorable member in the body of Christ.

Chapter Eighteen

A SHINING MODEL OF HUMILITY

St. John the Baptist is a humble giant and not only a prophet but more than a prophet in the words of the Lord Jesus. His great testimony honored St. John when He said, "Truly, I say to you, among those born of women there has not risen one greater than John the Baptist" (Matt. 11:11). Let's reflect on the Baptist's humility.

So what does humility mean? The term "humility" comes from the Latin word *humilitas*, and it drives from the word *humus*, meaning "earth." When we say someone is down to earth, we mean he or she is humble.

The virtue of John's great humility is evident when he declares to the disputing inquirers, "I am not the Christ, but I have been sent before Him" (John 3:28) and "He must increase, but I must decrease" (John 3:30). Earlier, in John 1:27, he says, "It is He who, coming after me, is preferred before me, whose sandal strap I am not worthy to loose." Today, we can emulate this giant in learning how to cultivate humility. Humility involves an outlook that focuses on things other than self-regard. It involves an accurate view of self. To attain humility, we ought to ponder what St. Augustine says: "Christ is the gate that is humble and low. All who want to enter by the gate must humble themselves and stoop low. Any who do not humble themselves, but make themselves important, are clearly proposing to enter by scaling the wall. But climbing the wall means heading for a fall."[9]

Praxis's distinct process and its explicit goal is to empower us to cultivate this virtue of humility. You could ask friends who you trust to honestly point out three things that they appreciate about you and three areas where you might need some growth. Listen and learn! Refrain from arguing or trying to refute a point. To have humility is to have an open mind. Anyone who seeks to cultivate this virtue should start any meeting with a question instead of giving instructions or proposing a solution. It takes humility to show what one does not know instead of what one does.

Accepting challenges without the fear of failure means to embrace one's life as it is rather than as one wishes it to be. Should you fail, learn from your mistakes, strive to do it better next time, and accept success and failure as part of life's journey. In addition, avoiding self-centeredness is crucial, let's learn from today's humble giant who knows his place and put it bluntly: "He who comes from above is above all; he who is of the earth is earthly and speaks of the earth" (John 3:31). Heeding the words of St. John the Baptist and cultivating humility could help us all be down-to-earth people.

To teach the virtue of humility to children, it is amazingly effective when parents do so by modeling. Never underestimate the power of teaching through example. Humility must be consistently modeled as a lifestyle. Parents will build their children up and help them by sharing with them their Christian beliefs and the example of our Lord Jesus, who says "learn from Me, for I am gentle and lowly in heart" (Matthew 11:29). It is always sad to witness parents reprimanding their children in the presence of strangers or in public places. Parents ought to refrain from humiliating their children but rather treat them with respect.

Such respectable conduct teaches the children to know and comprehend the Lord's empathy and learn to love Him and serve Him as well as serve the family, one another, the poor, and the homeless. Coach children to help them learn how to respond rather than to react, and show gratitude by saying "please" and "thank you." Should they make mistakes or hurt someone's feeling, teach them how to apologize. Sincere apology is a key component of humility. Finally, we all ought to be inspired by the one who the Lord says, "Among those born of women there has not risen one greater than John the Baptist."

Chapter Nineteen

LUKEWARM STATE AND LENT

I know your works, that you are neither cold nor
hot. I could wish you were cold or hot.
—Revelation 3:15

The Laodicean Church apparently was in a state of spiritual indifference, a lukewarm or half-hearted attitude toward faith. The word "Laodicean" is found in chapter 3, verses 15 and 16 of the book of Revelation in which the church of Laodicea is admonished for being "neither cold nor hot...but just lukewarm" in its devotion to the Lord. The name of that church had become a general term for any irresolute and hesitant follower of the Christian faith. In John's vision in the book of Revelation (Rev. 3:14), Christ instructs John to write a message to the seven churches of Asia Minor. The message to the Laodicean Church is one of judgment with a call to repentance. The Lord declares, "I could wish you were cold or hot...because you are lukewarm and neither cold nor hot, I will spew you out of My mouth" (Rev. 3:15–16).

Our attention then is brought to the root cause in the following verse: "Because you say, I am rich, have become wealthy, and have need of nothing—and do not know that you are wretched, miserable, poor, blind, and naked" (Rev. 3:17). The same warning is made today for our materialistic society and to those who practice their faith half-heartedly. Perhaps no passage is more relevant to reflect upon than Matthew 6:19–34, which deals with our pursuit of earthly treasures. Hence, some of us may be setting aside the true mission in life for which we have been called to fulfill. In other word, we favor activities and interests that Jesus simply describes as worrying about eating, drinking, and clothing and serving mammon rather than seeking first and foremost the kingdom of God and His righteousness.

In this regard, St. Maximus the Confessor explains precisely how to arrange a program that is in each person's capability and then concentrate on one's spiritual work. He states,

> Those who do not know how to walk in the way of the spirit are likely to fail to keep a watchful eye on the passions that rage within them, and let themselves entirely taken up by the body. Then they reach one of two opposites states. Either they become gluttonous, profligate, miserable, choleric, full of rancor, and this quenches their spirit, or they overdo the mortification and they lose their clarity of thought.[10]

Lent is the spring season of spiritual life and a time of renewal. The faithful ought to heed the guidance of St. Maximus and keep a watchful eye on passions, their worries to pursue earthly treasures, and illegitimate or coercive power. The Coptic Orthodox Church unites herself each year to the mystery of Jesus in the desert, who vanquished the tempter for us. This is the season of penance to start anew and leave behind once and for all the things that separate us from the Lord. To start anew, we ought to refrain from all distractions, from all anxieties about life and living. If the mind is preoccupied by two matters, it cannot give equal time to both. It will shift gears so that one gets the priority over the other.

During this penitential season, the faithful practice spending more time in an intimate relationship with the Lord. Aim to refrain from indulging in food or pleasurable activities and instead share your money and resources with those in need. Most importantly, to overcome the lukewarm state of spiritual life, we need to seek first the kingdom of God and His righteousness. By making the kingdom of God our treasure and having a clear understanding that this principle is at work, Jesus wants us, by faith, to choose to set our will to make God's kingdom our main priority. Even for those who think they have a higher calling serving His name, the Lord stops them in their track and asks them to pay attention to their devotion and their intimate relationship with Him, making the kingdom of God their utmost goal and highest treasure.

In our busy daily life, we often assume that God's main calling on our lives is to work for Him. But working for Christ should be secondary to our devotion to Him. To clarify further the importance of this, the Lord presents us with crucial yet significantly different aspects of serving and devotion. In the story of Mary and Martha, Jesus says, "Martha, Martha, you are worried and troubled about many things. But one thing is needed, and Mary has chosen the good part, which will not be taken away from her" (Luke 10:41–42). There is nothing wrong with serving, but Jesus is showing that service has to give way to worship. This is a gentle rebuke by Jesus urging Martha to leave her serving for the time being and concentrate on the more urgent responsibility. His words today are also a gentle rebuke urging us to leave whatever preoccupies us and seek first the kingdom of God and His righteousness, the most important treasure of all.

Finally, let's be vigilant in responding to the Laodicean call to be zealous and repent. "Behold, I stand at the door and knock. If anyone hears My voice and opens the door, I will come in to him and dine with him, and he with Me" (Rev. 3:20).

The Three Pillars of Lent

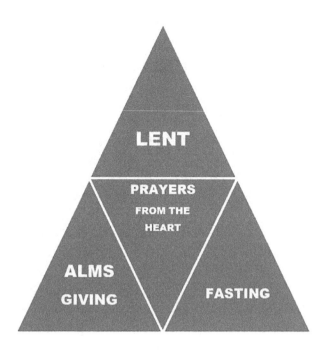

Prayer, fasting, and almsgiving are the three pillars of Lent that deepen our commitment to God's love, because they involve our relationships with God, self, and others.

Chapter Twenty

UTILIZE STRATEGY AND
WIN THE WAR

*Put on the whole armor of God, that you may be
able to stand against the wiles of the devil.*
—Ephesians 6:11

No wonder! For Satan himself is transformed into an angel of light.
—2 Corinthians 11:14

To win a war against Satan, we must utilize the Lord's strategy and be prepared to know the enemy's tactics, for he is a deceiver. Every person of faith should not be overconfident and never underestimate the enemy in a spiritual war. The faithful need to build strong alliances based on trust and confidence in our Lord. Remember, achieving success depends on walking in the footsteps of our master. Thus, ensure that you are fighting for the truth and justice to win with integrity by adopting the Savior's plan and avoiding failure and the need for repentance. Spiritual strength is achieved by living a sacramental life and sanctifying grace. An enlightened brain and diligent soul are always superior to brawn and self-trust.

We heard how Satan dared to tempt Jesus over two thousand years ago. But surely it is not only about the encounter between the tempter and the Lord; it is also about how the Lord wants to prepare us to fight the good fight in the here and now. It is about the battle of facing the evil of sin every day in our life. Sin severs the profound relation of man to God. The unmasked true identity of sin is rejection of God and opposition to Him. You may ask, where does evil come from? St. Augustine pondered this very question and thought to find a solution when he stated, "I sought whence evil comes and there was no solution." His own painful quest would only be resolved by his conversion to a life in service to God.

The reality of sin is revealed only in the light of the death and resurrection of Jesus Christ. We must know Christ as the source of grace in order to know Adam as the source of sin. To enter the battle and overcome evil—lust of the flesh; pride; satanic plots; lust for riches, power, and prestige—we must equip ourselves with grace and His written word. This exactly what the Lord Jesus did in conquering the evil one.

Satan tempted Christ to seek immediate gain through deceitful and devious tactics. He wanted Christ to turn stone into bread, to cast Himself off the pinnacle of the temple, and to fall down and worship him. In every case, Jesus turned Satan back by quoting scripture. So let's learn and follow by example. When Jesus responds to the three temptations of the devil in the wilderness, he quotes from Deuteronomy. "Man shall not live by bread alone" (Matt. 4:4, Deut. 8:3); "You shall not tempt the Lord your God" (Matt. 4:7, Deut. 6:16); and "You shall worship the Lord your God, and Him only you shall serve" (Matt. 4:10, Deut. 6:13).

Lust of the flesh can be healed by fasting. Fasting more than anything else reveals what controls us and what we are obsessed with. Those who long to be transformed into the image of the Lord Jesus will reap the amazing benefit of fasting. It cultivates humility. The psalmist David said, "I chastened my soul with fasting" (Ps. 69:10). With humility one is able to control anger and all other ill feelings we may have, such as envy, jealously, maliciousness, and fear. In fact, the most powerful weapon against sexual impurity is humility. By fasting, we rely on God's word more than anything else. Fasting and humility can liberate those who are shackled by lust and sexual impurity.

Again, Satan tempted Christ to call upon His Father's power and protection just as he usually tempts men to pride and presumption even in holy places. The Lord again rebuked him and turned him back by quoting the scripture in response to his misquoted words. Finally, Christ was tempted to worship Satan, but he rejected the proposal with abhorrence: "Away with you, Satan" (Matthew 4:10)! Some temptations are wicked and must be rejected at once. It is good to be quick in resisting temptation. If we resist the devil, he will flee from us.

We learn from the Lord's example how to overcome and conquer satanic temptations and his alluring tactics. Fasting, prayer, and almsgiving are pillars of the faith, especially during Lent. However, they are only a means to an end. The purpose of Lent is conversion—a total conversion in which we have an intimate relationship with the Lord. There is, however, a battle to be fought daily with three enemies—lust of the flesh, Satan, and the world—and we have to remain sober and diligent.

THE VOICE OF CHRIST

I taught the prophets from the beginning,
and even to this day I continue to speak to all
men. But many are hardened. Many are deaf
to My voice. Most men listen more willingly
to the world than to God. They are more
ready to follow the appetite of their flesh than
the good pleasure of God. The world, which
promises small and passing things, is served
with great energies: I promise great and eternal
things and the hearts of men grow dull.[11]

Chapter Twenty-One

AN EXTRAORDINARY WOMAN!

"I know that Messiah, is coming... When he
comes, he will tell us all things."
—John 4:25

The extraordinary Samaritan woman is recorded only in the Gospel of John. There is nothing mentioned about her name or age. However, her encounter and conversation with Jesus at the well is the longest one-on-one chat recorded in the scriptures. Jesus asked for a drink of water; on the surface he apparently was thirsty. After all, he had just sat down beside Jacob's well in the midday heat. But while Jesus is thirsty for water, he is thirstier for the woman's salvation. St. Augustine wrote: "Although Jesus asked for a drink, His real thirst was for this woman's faith." This leads us to meditate on His thirsting not only at the well but also again when he is hanging on the cross. His last words at the crucifixion were: "*I thirst.*"

The Lord is thirsty for the salvation of mankind. Thirsty for our love and intimate attachment to Him. Thirsty to share His love and to go forth and bring the good news to other people. The Samaritan woman's story follows on the heels of Jesus's interaction with Nicodemus (John 3:1–21). He was a Pharisee and prominent member of the Jewish Sanhedrin. In spite of the similarities in the two meetings between Nicodemus and the Samaritan woman, there are differences in the way Jesus unveiled the truth to them. While Nicodemus needed to see himself as a sinner in order to understand the divine presence of the Son of Man, the Samaritan woman, who knew she was a sinner, needed to see herself as a person of worth and value. Hence, this provides us with one of the most powerful lessons in all of scripture.

This story teaches us that God finds us worthy of His love in spite of our sinful nature and wasted lives. Many of the faithful are nowadays too busy even to spend a little time with Him, while Jesus is saying the same words personally to many of us: *"I thirst."* Would we ever find ourselves responding to satisfy His thirst by giving Him our love and sharing that love with our neighbor? God values us enough to actively seek us, and that is exactly what He did with the Samaritan woman. As a result of Jesus's conversation, only a person like the Samaritan woman—who had lived a dubious life, an outcast from her own people—could understand what this means. To be wanted, to be cared for when apparently no one, not even herself, could see anything of value in her—this is grace indeed.

This amazing encounter emphasizes the fact that only through Jesus can we obtain and receive eternal life: "Jesus answered, 'Whoever drinks of this water will thirst again, but whoever drinks of the water I shall give him will never thirst. But the water that I shall give him will become in him a fountain of water springing up into everlasting life'" (John 4:13–14)… "And those who worship God, worship Him in spirit and truth" (John 4:24)… "The woman said to Him, 'I know that Messiah is coming' (who is called Christ)…Jesus said to her, 'I who speak to you am He'" (John 4: 25–26). Then we learn that the Lord's primary focus is not on food but on doing the will of His Father. In contrast, Satan is the ultimate example of one who did not want the will of God but asserted his will against God's will (Isa. 14:12–15). This teaches us to set our priorities straight. Before doing any worthwhile deeds, even serving needy souls, first and foremost one must focus on doing the will of God.

Again, in this wonderful encounter with the Samaritan woman, the Lord teaches us not to procrastinate, thinking things simply take time and therefore one cannot avoid the waiting. Instead, we must be diligent and look at the fields, "for they are already white for harvest" (John 4:35). The idea of harvest means there are many people ready to be received in the kingdom of God. His disciples should see themselves as workers and reapers in the harvest. Those who reap receive wages and gather fruit for eternal life. Thus, those who sows with the Lord and those who reap may rejoice together.

Finally, many of the Samaritans from that town came to believe in Jesus because of the woman's testimony: "He told me all that I ever did" (John 4:39). The woman told everyone about Jesus, suggesting that He might be the Messiah. After Jesus's death and resurrection, the disciples went and told people about Him because they were sent to do so. The Samaritan woman did the same thing, but on her own initiative. She saw what should be done and did it. No wonder she is considered by many as the first apostle. As people of faith, we could learn to do the same.

THE VOICE OF CHRIST
My CHILD, hear My words, words of
greatest sweetness surpassing all
the knowledge of the philosophers
and wise men of earth. My words
are spirit and life, and they are not to
be weighed by man's understanding.
They are not to be invoked in vanity
but are to be heard in silence, and
accepted with all humility and
with great affection. [12]

Chapter Twenty-Two

SUFFERING GUILT AND SHAME!

Guilt and shame involve negatively judging oneself when one believes he has failed to live up to the standard of other people. No doubt that the parents of the blind man suffered guilt and shame because of their son's blindness and the perceived sin involved. Even when the parents saw their son miraculously gain his sight, they were unable to celebrate such a miracle. They could not admit the miracle occurred, because they lived in fear of the Pharisees. They feared the agony of facing accusations and the threat of being cast out from the synagogue. It is clear that the blind man's parents not only suffered tremendously during this ordeal but also throughout their lives raising a disabled child who had to beg for his livelihood.

The experience of the blind man's parents leads us to reflect on guilt and shame, as both are harsh feelings that cause so much unnecessary suffering. Paralyzing shame can lead a person to feel unworthy and undermine a sense of security, or it can simply make one feel less than others. It causes the person to experience intense discomfort and feelings of inadequacy among family members, friends, and others. The person who suffers from these feelings tends to isolate and withdraw by a desire to hide. Shame, guilt, and embarrassment can lead to anxiety and depression. However, guilt also can be healthy in moving a believer to alleviate the sense of guilt via penance and confession.

Many parents nowadays are experiencing these feelings raising their children in what amounts to a promiscuous environment. They wonder how their children will turn out and how they will survive in a society of declining morals. Over the past five decades, our society has become secularized and is determined to separate people from the moral standards rooted in the Bible. As a result, teaching moral values has been absent from schools since the 1960s and has virtually disappeared from the culture and fabric of our nation.

The hope now rests within the family and the church. Both are vital in developing children's morals and building Christian character within them. This is the true path for children to learn how to make moral decisions in difficult situations. However, violence, drug use, and now school shootings—a rapidly growing problem—have become rampant. It is true what has been said: America's failure to protect its children from drugs, bullying, and violence is a national disgrace.

Now imagine if the family of the blind man suffered humiliation and guilt despite them not doing anything wrong. Similarly, think how millions of students and their parents feel witnessing and experiencing the moral decay of the nation. Those in authority have failed to protect thousands of children from violence, drugs, and even murder on school grounds. Therefore, it is time to join together and defend our children. It is time to rise up and learn to be bold like the blind man facing the Jewish leaders, proclaiming our faith as the way we walk it, not only talk it. We need to declare the truth in deed and creed and live an abundant life.

It is time to teach our children not to panic and fall victim to these violent acts but to call on the mighty Lord to protect them and give them courage wherever they are. It is time to teach our children that life is not guaranteed and no one knows when or where life will end, and we better be prepared at all times to meet the Lord. Jesus's life is proof of that—death and resurrection teach us the Christian principle that death is the door to life, that suffering is the way to glory. This is the path Jesus took—should his followers expect anything less?

It is time for parents to be kind and loving to their children and to one another so their children grow with peace of heart and mind and not be angry at them and society as a whole. It is time for the family to be mindful of the presence of the Lord and ask Him to reveal to the faithful the blind spots in each familial relationship. We do this so we may be enlightened, just as the Lord restored sight to the blind man and enlightened him to vindicate himself and shame those who were spiritually blind.

AT THE EYE NEEDS LIGHT
To see visible objects we need the eyes of
the body. To understand intelligible truth
We need the eyes of the mind. To have the
vision of divine things we cannot do
without faith. What the eye is for the body,
faith is for reason. To be more precise;
the eye needs the light which puts it in
contact with visible things; reason needs
faith to show divine things.[13]

—St. Theodoret

Chapter Twenty-Three

THE DEITY OF CHRIST!

The Sunday after Easter is known as the Sunday of St. Thomas. Liturgically, the church remembers the apostle Thomas who was ashamed of his unbelief and cried out, "My Lord and my God." Upon seeing the resin Christ, he was told to reach his finger, look at the Lord's hands, and "reach your hand here and put it into My side" (John 20:27).

However, as we examine the scripture, we realize there is a bigger picture to this event. St. Maximus the Confessor says the following about the sacred scripture: "It contains the letter, the visible text, which is transitory. But it also contains the spirit hidden beneath the letter, and this is never extinguished and this ought to be the object of our contemplation."[14] Thus, within the text of this scripture's passage we find one of the most powerful and direct pieces of evidence for the doctrine of the *deity* of Christ, or the belief that Jesus is fully human and fully divine united in one. The disbelief of the apostle furnished us with a full and satisfactory demonstration of the resurrection of our Lord.

Second, the Lord teaches us to believe, and He blessed those who have not seen and yet have believed. Third, contemplating these fundamental beliefs and values is essential to any relationship's growth and lasting potential, especially with the Lord as well as with those who we care for. Anytime we are having doubts about a relationship, let's rest assured the answers we seek are within us. St. Paul says, "Even though our outward man is wasting away, our inner nature is being renewed every day" (2 Cor. 4:16), and we should not allow fear or doubt to muffle our inner voice.

Most importantly, today we ought to live a joyous life celebrating and proclaiming the risen Christ as well as His outpouring of love for us now and forever. Let's encourage each other to continue to carry His love in our hearts and share it with one another! That is truly the big picture and the crux of the matter.

I read an inspirational message by Christine Caine reflecting on Psalm 34:3: "Oh, magnify the LORD with me, and let us exalt His name together." She shared that while she was student, her professor at the university projected an image of a small black dot in the middle of a big white screen. Then he asked his students, "What do you see?" Every student immediately responded, "A black dot." He paused and then asked again, "What do you see?" When the students gave the same reply, he told them that he saw a huge white space. In other words, while they saw a small dot, he saw something far bigger. It had been there all along, but each one of his students had missed it.

The moral of the story is that we often see what our eyes are trained to see, and it takes effort and time to train them otherwise. How often do we focus on the small things in life instead of the larger God that we serve? We can have twenty great things happening in our lives, but when one thing does not go right, we lose sight of the twenty and focus on the one little black dot.

This is why we must always decide to make God bigger than anything else in our lives. The more we focus on Him, the smaller the dots will become! Caine added that we should then learn to shift our focus and shout with the psalmist, "Hallelujah! Let's make Him bigger. Let's magnify our King!" And you make Him bigger by fixing your eyes on Him and not on fear, insecurity, doubt, or conflict in your life.

When we do that, when we shift our perspective to focus on God, faith will rise in our heart, and we will live knowing the truth that we serve a big God who can do big things!

Chapter Twenty-Four

CELESTIAL NATURE BEINGS

Celestial beings tend to float in a spiritual realm. They find themselves privileged to witness glorious life above and beyond earthly life unknown to the average human eye. They have a natural intuition and may have an "unveiled eye." They can have visions that belong to the spirit world, things of a heavenly nature. St. Paul speaks of visions and revelations of the Lord and says, "I know a man in Christ who fourteen years ago—whether in the body I do not know, or whether out of the body I do not know, God knows—such one was caught up to the third heaven...how he was caught up into paradise and heard inexpressible words, which it is not lawful for a man to utter" (2 Cor. 12:2–4).

St. John, the author of Revelation, had similar vision and says that on the Lord's Day he was "in Spirit" and heard behind him a loud voice "like a trumpet" saying, "I am the Alpha and the Omega, the First and the Last" (Rev. 1:10–11). This celestial experience is also found in Exodus (3:4), when Moses heard God calling him from within the bush, "Moses! Moses!" and he answered, "Here I am." And when Moses asked God what would he should say to the Israelites if they ask what is God's name (3:14), God says to Moses, "I AM WHO I AM." Therefore, it behooves us to reflect on scripture as the Lord speaks of a sacred mystery of a divine nature that requires a supernatural explanation. He says, "I am the bread of life" (John 6:35).

The Lord used the same phrase "I am" in seven declarations about Himself. In all seven, He spells out His journey on earth and expresses His saving relationship toward the world. All appear in the book of John. This is a phenomenal statement! First by equating Himself with bread, Jesus is saying He is essential for life. Second, the life Jesus is referring to is not just physical life but eternal life as well. Jesus is trying to draw the Jews out from their physical realm and into the spiritual realm. He is contrasting what He had done feeding the five thousand the bread He miraculously created the day before. That was physical bread that perishes. He is spiritual bread that gives eternal life.

Third, and very importantly, Jesus is declaring another truth regarding his divinity. That means God the Son, the preexisting divine *logos* taking a human body and human nature, "was made flesh" and conceived in the womb of Mary the Theotokos. The phrase "I am" is the covenant name of God (Yahweh), revealed to Moses at the burning bush (Exod. 3:14), "IAM WHO I AM."

Finally, consider the remarkable words "come" and "believe." "He who comes to Me shall never hunger, and he who believes in Me shall never thirst" (John 6:35). Coming to Jesus involves making a choice to forsake the world and follow Him. Believing in Jesus means placing our faith in Him, believing that He is who He says He is, that He will do what He says He will do, and that He is the only one who can.

What does that all mean to all of us, myself included? As believers trusting the Lord for our salvation and eternal life, we are members in the body of Christ (1 Cor. 12:27). For the body to be healthy and performs well, we must be united working together and loving one another. As a single body, we all have spiritual gifts God has given us, and we all should be involved in supporting, guiding, strengthening, and consoling each other. A believer will never reach full spiritual maturity unless he or she is on the road to perfection, investing in God's talents and gifts. We all surely need the support and encouragement of other body members (1 Cor. 12:21–26).

Therefore, church attendance, participation, and fellowship ought to be religiously adhered to and be part of the faithful's life. The life of the church and the body of Christ should prompt a sense of belonging and a desire to worship God, receive His word, and live a life of fellowship with Him.

Just as Jesus is the cornerstone of the church (1 Peter 2:6), we are "like living stones" as well, being built in a spiritual house to be holy people, offering worship to God through Jesus Christ (1 Peter 2:5). When we participate in the sacrament of the most holy Eucharist, we are united in body and blood together with the soul and divinity of our Lord Jesus Christ. Then and only then do we live and move as spiritual beings devoted to the glory of God and live above and beyond the temporal world and its fears, temptations, and distractions.

Reflecting on being spiritual beings united in the body of Christ partaking of the most holy Eucharist, the late Bishop Gregory said,

> Without this union, the believer cannot produce the fruits of the Holy Spirit. But he, who receives the sacrament regularly and worthy, will have Christ dwelling as a king in the heart. He drives away all his enemies and manifests himself to him (John 14:21). He gradually reveals to him the light of his glory and divinity to the degree that his inner eye can tolerate. With frequent participation in the Eucharist, the human heart glows with bright light that is sometimes reflected on his face. However, the inner light is enough to change him into a *celestial being* whose eye is always pure and his thoughts holy. The light that has erupted inside him has made him partaker of the divine nature.[15]

Chapter Twenty-Five

TRULY HOW MUCH DO
WE KNOW HIM?

"Come and see" (John 1:46). This was Philip's own answer to Nathanael when he asked him, "Can anything good come out of Nazareth?" Philip was among the first to be called (John 1:43) and yet had not learned to know the Christ. So he said, "Lord, show us the Father, and it is sufficient for us." Jesus said to him, "Have I been with you so long, and yet you have not known Me, Philip? He who has seen Me has seen the Father; so how can you say, 'Show us the Father'" (John 14:8–9)?

Philip had been with the Lord for a long time and heard all He had said of Himself as the door, the Good Shepherd, the Son of God, the Son of Man, the light of the world, the bread of life, the living water, the way, the truth, and the life. He'd also been witness to mighty miracles and signs, yet still Philip apparently did not fully comprehend the deity of Christ.

There is in our Lord's words a tone of tender reproach and surprise. Philip, who had followed Him from the first, shows by this question that he did not even know that Jesus and His Father were one and that those who have seen the Son have seen the Father. Nor did Philip know His purpose and mission. This speaks perhaps to many Christian today, including preachers and theologians. It is possible that men who appear to be near to Christ have never discovered the depth, purpose, and mission of Christ's life.

In this encounter with Philip, the Lord reveals and affirms what He has been saying all along. His boundless and sacrificial love has brought Him from the bosom of His Father in heaven to save us and lift us up with Him to be with Him in eternal life. "No one has seen God at any time. The only begotten Son, who is in the bosom of the Father, He has declared Him" (John 1:18).

However, Christ's answer is truly comforting not only to the disciples but to all who believe in Him, including each one of us. It boldly declares that He is in the Father and the Father in Him. Christ lives, and so do we! Death will come for all of us, yet it has no power over us, for the risen Christ is a guarantee that we will go on living as He does. We shall have eternal life in Christ. The joy of the resurrection morning is for us the joy of knowing that we have life in Him. "Whoever eats My flesh and drinks My blood has eternal life, and I will raise him up at the last day" and "He who eats My flesh and drinks My blood abides in Me and I in him" (John 6:54, 56).

Thus, even at the point of departure from earthly life and seemingly being enveloped by the shadow of the death, Christ shall not cease as an operative principle. Rather, we shall continue on in the hereafter to the making of our earth fit for the coming of the kingdom of God. That is His promise who said, "Because I live, ye shall live also" (John 14:19).

In the book *God Calling*, the Lord Jesus reveals the following about those who've departed earthly life:

> Your loved ones are very safe in MY keeping. Learning, loving and working, theirs is a life of happiness and progress. They live to serve and serve they will truly do. They serve Me and those they love. Ceaselessly they serve. But their ministrations, so many, so diverse, you see no more than those in My time on earth in human form could have seen the angels who ministered unto Me in the wilderness. How often mortals rush to earthly friends who can serve them in so limited a way, when the friends who are freed from the

limitations of humanity can serve them so much better, understand better, protect better, plan better, and even plead better their cause with Me. You do well to remember your friends in the Unseen. Companying with them the more you live in this Unseen World the gentler will be your passing when it comes… "And this is Life Eternal that we may know Thee, the Only True God, and Jesus Christ whom Thou has sent." Learning to know Me draws that Kingdom very near, and in Me, and through knowledge of Me, the dear ones there become very near and dear."[16]

The introduction to *God calling* states it is "not a regular book as any other book, for it does not contain words of a human being, but the words of the Lord Jesus. Through its daily message, it reveals the Lord's heart and His paternal Love toward our pitiful world, offering the curative healing to every wounded heart groaning in pain."

***

** *God Calling* was published in Arabic by the Coptic Orthodox Church of Alexandria, with a foreword by HG Bishop Boutros. It was translated by Dr. Samir Tenagho, professor and chair of the Department of Civil Law, College of Law, Alexandria University.

Chapter Twenty-Six

TREASURES OF THE HEART

"A good man out of the good treasure of the heart brings forth good; and an evil man out of the evil treasure of his heart brings forth evil" (Luke 6:45). But what is the definition of a good man? He is one who has been newly created in Christ, a true believer, a sincere lover of Him, who follows Him and serves Him. Every Christian person may think that because they are a Christian, then they are good, and that may be true…until we listen to what they truly say and see how they truly behave. Then and only then would you know what kind of a person he or she is!

The mouth speaks what the heart is full of. That is how Jesus condemned the Pharisees when He said to them, "Brood of vipers! How can you being evil, speak good things? For out of the abundance of the heart the mouth speaks" (Matt. 12:34). Jesus warns us not only about the manner in which we express ourselves but also about idle words. He said, "But I say to you that for every idle word men may speak, they will give account on the day of judgment" (Matt. 12:36). Idle words are undisciplined, empty speech. Ephesians 5:4 provides a partial list of idle speech, including obscenity, foolish talking, and inappropriately coarse jesting.

The manner in which we express ourselves is a measure of where we stand in our spiritual life. The words we use should never be meaningless, empty, or full of fury, nor should we have an apathetic attitude or react with antipathy, dislike, or animosity. We should be full only of empathy and understanding for others and be respectful of their perspectives regardless of how they may differ from our own. That is what we call strength formed by humility and gentleness.

"Whoever guards his mouth preserves his life, but he who opens wide his lips shall have destruction" (Prov. 13:3).

Speaking of words, Fred Rogers (1928–2003) a Presbyterian minister and the host of the preschool television series *Mister Rogers' Neighborhood* for more than three decades, once said,

> Most of us, I believe, admire strength. It's something we tend to respect in others, desire for ourselves, and wish for our children. Sometimes, though, I wonder if we confuse strength and other words, like aggression and even violence. Real strength is neither male nor female but is, quite simply, one of the finest characteristics that any human being can possess.

Real strength is truly reflected in the gentleness of the soul, because it remains constant and clear-minded across all manner of situations. Gentleness breeds peace, calm, and consistency of character. It is not volatile or abrupt in its response to the world. Gentleness, kindness, and self-control are some of the fruits of the Holy Spirit.

Christ has given us the privilege to be His own and trust in Him. Someone once said, "Knowing Christ died—that is history. Believing He died for me—that is salvation." Only when we follow His commandments to love the Father and our neighbor do we become His children, His friends, His servants, and members of His spiritual kingdom. St. Clement of Alexandria says,

> The perfect person does good through love. His actions are not motivated by desire for personal benefits, so he does not have personal advantage as his aim. But as soon he has realized the beauty of doing good, he does it with all his energies and in all that he does... The rule of life for a perfect person is to be the image and likeness of God.[17]

BOOK TWO

GREAT CHARACTER TRANSFORMATION

Learning from saintly giants
Living through their world experiencing their lives!

Chapter One

AN ALIENATED SOUL

Nothing is more difficult or unbearable than to feel alienated, isolated, estranged, or ignored by friends and others. Nothing is harsher, more devastating, and crueler than for one or both spouses in a marriage to feel alienated, ignored, or rejected. Nothing is more sad, destabilizing, and destructive than parents who neglect, degrade, or abuse their children.

That is the subject of the following Gospel story. A man named Zacchaeus was a chief tax collector who was rich, yet he felt rejected and hated by his own people because they considered him a corrupt extortionist and a sinner. As such, tax collectors were cast out of the community and could not even worship in the synagogue. They were not welcomed in any social relationships because people wouldn't go near them, as they were considered unclean, and anybody who came near a tax collector would be defiled. In other words, Zacchaeus was an isolated, alienated, and lonely soul and all his riches left him empty and abandoned.

That was how the people felt about Zacchaeus and all sinners, but not Jesus. He boldly declared in Luke's Gospel, "For the Son of Man has come to seek and to save that which was lost" (Luke 19:10). That statement of our Lord Jesus is the most glorious, most important, and most valuable truth ever revealed in scripture. Why? Because God has always been a seeker and a saver of those who are lost. This is true to the nature of God. Jesus did not come into the world to set Himself as king of Israel or to restore justice and world peace. Nor did he come to merely heal the sick or feed the hungry and perform miracles. He didn't even come simply to set Himself as a model for living a moral life.

Jesus came into this world to give His very life to save ours. Like Zacchaeus, we all are sinners in desperate need of salvation. Apart of Jesus, we will die in our sins (John 8:24). Only Jesus is the answer; He has the solution, the cure for our sins. He came to give eternal life to anyone who would believe in Him. That is the Christian message. That is the only Christian message. Everything in the Old Testament prophesied to that end. Everything in the New Testament speaks to its truth.

St. Luke wonderfully illustrates the image of the Lord as a seeker and savior. In Luke 15:4–32, he reminds us that God likens Himself to a shepherd seeking a lost sheep, a woman seeking a lost coin, and a father seeking a lost son. This is God, the shepherd, who goes after the lost sheep who is in grave danger.

> And when he has found it, he lays it on his shoulders rejoicing, comes home, calls together his friends and neighbors saying to them, "Rejoice with me, for I have found my sheep which was lost." I say to you likewise, there will be more joy in heaven over one sinner who repents than over ninety-nine righteous persons who need no repentance. (Luke 15:5–7)

God does it for His own joy. He does it for His own glory.

And Jesus did it for Zacchaeus. He goes to his house because He seeks to save this lost man. He is on a divine mission and a divine timetable. He knows exactly who Zacchaeus is and where He is going to meet him. He is the lonely rejected man who desired to see Jesus, who ran ahead and climbed into a sycamore tree just to see Him. Little did he know that he had an appointment with salvation. Zacchaeus received Him gladly, gave half of his goods to the poor, and restored fourfold for anything taken by false accusation. There Jesus said to him, "Today salvation has come to this house, because he also is a son of Abraham" (Luke 19:9) What a contrast with the people of Israel, who began to grumble when they witnessed this. All the way to the end, they're holding on to their vile and self-righteous attitude while Jesus is saving sinners. He has not come to call the righteous but the sinners to repentance.

In his writings, St. Theodoret speaks of how the Lord chose to demonstrate the holiness of His providential care, stating, "The Lord of the world did not consider it right to allow human beings, for the love of whom everything had been made, to be besieged by sin and to be sold like slaves to death. Undoubtedly the reason he assumed human form, hid his invisible nature under visible guise, and kept the visible nature free from the stain of sin."[18]

Chapter Two

THE EMPTY TOMB!

For more than two centuries, Americans have celebrated the Thanksgiving holiday. The celebration began with the Pilgrims in Plymouth, Massachusetts, who in 1621 called it their "First Thanksgiving" with the Native Americans who helped them survive that first year in the New World. Today, however, there is too little gratitude among the college-age population for living in the most prosperous and free country in the history of the world.

During the third week of November 2018, a national news reporters visited some campuses to interview college students about Thanksgiving. Many responded that they had stopped celebrating Thanksgiving once they got to college, and before that they had been lukewarm on the idea. When the reporter inquired why they wouldn't celebrate a national holiday, he was told it was because they did not believe in who they should give thanks to. In other words, they actually didn't believe in a god to give thanks to.

No wonder Thanksgiving has been labeled as a "turkey day." Another label is "Black Thursday," and it has nothing to do with Black Friday, the shopping day that comes after Thanksgiving. The group United American Indians of New England consider Thanksgiving to be a national day of mourning due to countless atrocities committed against indigenous tribes by the Puritans.

When President George Washington made the Thanksgiving proclamation back on October 3, 1789, in New York City, he started with the sentence, "Whereas it is the duty of all Nations to acknowledge the providence of Almighty God, to obey his will, to be grateful for his benefits, and humbly to implore his protection and favor." On Thanksgiving Day this year, when our family sat at the dinner table, my daughter thought we all should speak about what we were thankful for. Each one of us had many things to be thankful for, and we usually say that we ought to be thankful not only on Thanksgiving Day but on every day, as our Coptic Church taught us to do daily if not hourly.

The scriptures remind us that we all ought to be thankful for the most important thing of all, and that is "the empty tomb." For if the tomb of Jesus of Nazareth was not found empty after His crucifixion, then Christianity is the greatest lie in history. The apostle Paul says, "If Christ is not risen, your faith is futile; and you are still in your sins" (1 Cor. 15:17)!

Every day and even every hour in so many places in this country and abroad, we meet people who don't believe in resurrection and salvation through Jesus Christ. Why? Because it means they would be accountable to God and called to turn from their sin and trust the saving work of Jesus on the cross. So people reject the resurrection because to accept and believe it and live in the light of its reality means they must abandon their sinful lifestyles, and they don't want to do that.

The empty tomb declared the resurrection of our Lord. That day was the greatest event of all time. Nothing has so powerfully affected human thought more than Christ's resurrection. The night before, the guards were ordered to secure Jesus's tomb, and no one else dared to be there. All was quiet, still as death, except for the flickering flame of the soldiers' fire. "And, behold, there was a great earthquake: for the angel of the Lord descended from heaven, and came and rolled back the stone, and sat on it. His countenance was like lightning and his clothing as white as snow: and the guards shook for fear of him, and became like dead men" (Matt. 28:2–4). The angel then said to the women who came to the tomb bringing the spices, "He is not here; for He is risen, as He said. Come, see the place where the Lord lay. And go quickly and tell His disciples that He is risen from the dead. And indeed He is going before you into Galilee; there you will see Him. Behold I have told you" (Matt. 28:6–7).

In the words of St. Cyril of Jerusalem,

> He died, but he did not remain, as all human beings do, in the underworld. He is the only one free among the dead. The Savior becomes all things to all, according to the need for each: to those who ask for joy, he becomes the vine; to those who wish to enter, he becomes the door; to those who are under the weight of sin, he becomes a lamb. A lamb slain for them. He becomes all things to all, but he remains nonetheless what he is. He is called by a twofold name: Jesus because he gives us salvation, and Christ because he is priest. He is the healer of bodies and doctor of souls.[19]

Chapter Three

THE COST OF DISCIPLESHIP

In religious circles today—especially in Sunday schools—many church leaders enthusiastically encourage the faithful to become disciples of our Lord and serve Him. No one can underestimate the benefits and the blessings of being a disciple. But we hardly speak about the true cost of discipleship. Therefore, it is imperative that we first sit and count the cost; otherwise we find ourselves discouraged and faltering in the way, thus parting from the path of fellowship and the company of our Lord. We find in the Bible, when great multitudes went with Him, He turned and said to them, "If anyone comes to Me and does not hate his father and mother, wife and children, brothers and sisters, yes his own life also, he cannot be My disciple" (Luke 14:26).

Whom do we love? A father, a mother, wife and children, brothers and sisters, yes, and even our precious life—if we do not hate them all, we cannot be His disciple! How that could be? The commandments teach us to honor our parents. "Honor your father and your mother, that your days may be long in the land which the Lord your God is giving you" (Exod. 20:12).

The crux of the matter is that in order to be a disciple, our love for the Savior has to have precedence over any other human relationship. We must be willing to give up everything for the Lord Jesus. Therefore, if our parents will not follow Jesus, or even if they disown us for being Christians, we must still choose Him over them. It is in this sense that we "hate" our family members who reject the Lord or reject us because of the Lord. This is not easy, and of course it is right that we should love our family members and want them to love and follow God. After all, St. John says, "Beloved, let us love one another, for love is of God; and everyone who loves is born of God and knows God. He who does not love does not know God for God is love" (John 4:7–8).

The Lord Jesus may have chosen the word "hate" to show us that this is how parents might perceive the actions of a child who chooses the Lord above them. They will see it as disloyal and hateful, especially if the child tries to witness to them. The love of a Christian for a non-Christian is almost always seen as hatred, intolerance, bigotry, and so forth. But we must bear in mind what the Lord means when He says the world will hate us. Actually, the unbelieving relatives are part of the world, and Jesus said, "If the world hates you, you know that it hated Me before it hated you" (John 15:18).

Second, we must carry our own cross (Luke 14:27). The Lord Jesus here is looking at the process of daily death of the ego, of selfish desires, and of the willingness to bear reproach for His name's sake. So why was Jesus prompting cross bearing? Because He wanted disciples who were willing to face the difficulties it would take to serve Him. And not only to serve Him but to be willing to lay down their lives for the name of Jesus. We all know the history of Christianity, especially in the Coptic Church, who've witnessed and recorded her children not only being persecuted and oppressed but also shedding their blood as martyrs through the centuries and until this present day.

Because of His boundless love, the Lord was verbally abused, whipped, tortured, and crucified for the Gospel he proclaimed and for the sacrifice he offered for our sins. He paid the ultimate price for us. All Christians will suffer in this life and bear the reproach of Christ. St. Paul calls this filling up that which is lacking in Christ's affliction" (Col. 1:24). But how is this possible that Christians are filling up for what is lacking in Christ affliction? Christ's suffering lacks nothing, He suffers as the head of the church and gave the ultimate sacrifice—His life on the cross. Since we are member of His body, all of us are thus suffering in this life as well. So as members of the body of Christ, "Let love be without hypocrisy. Abhor what is evil. Cling to what is good. Be kindly affectionate to one another with brotherly love, in honor giving preference to one another" (Rom. 12:9–10).

To truly follow Christ, we must consider the cost of discipleship. He warns us not to begin to follow Him superficially, only to turn back later when things get tough. Great multitudes went along with Him; that is why He turned to them and laid out these demands of discipleship and its costs.

Making the decision to follow Him entails careful, detailed, rational choice, not an impulsive one made in the spur of the moment without much thought about the consequences. We must "sit down first and count the cost," referring to the man building the tower (Luke 14:28), and "sit down and take counsel," referring to the king considering going to war (Luke 14:31). And as Jesus says, "So likewise, whoever of you does not forsake all that he has cannot be My disciple" (Luke 14:33)

These are the prerequisites for the costs that He spells out. Again, let us remind ourselves the task is great, but it is extremely important and eternally rewarding. We ought not to fear, for His love is great and His grace will suffice and help us reach our destiny.

Chapter Four

OBEDIENCE AND SUBMISSION

After nine months and eight days, Zacharias's "mouth was opened and his tongue loosed, and he spoke, praising God" (Luke 1:64). Zacharias and his wife, Elizabeth, "were both righteous before God, walking in all the commandments and ordinances of the Lord blameless." Why then was Zacharias, a priestly and obedient man, told by the angel Gabriel, "Behold, you will be mute and not able to speak until the day these things take place" (Luke 1:20)? The answer is because of his lack of obedience and disbelief! He questioned the angel: "How shall I know this? For I am an old man, and my wife is well advanced in years" (Luke 1:18).

Obedience is a wonderful virtue that we ought to teach our children. The Lord demands it when He says, "Behold, I set before you today a blessing and a curse: the blessing, if you obey the commandments of the Lord your God, and the curse if you do not obey the commandments of the Lord your God" (Deut. 11:26–28). St. Mary is holy because she is fully obedient to the will of God. She freely unites her will with God's so that it affirms not her own good but the good of all His children as well. Mary—the "fiat" or "let it be done"—is our mother, truly a universal mother.

From the story of Zacharias's encounter with the angel, there are two lessons for us to learn:

First, Obedience Must Be Fulfilled

Submission to God's authority should be fulfilled. Mediocre obedience will "mute" our faith. It's only after we have fulfilled our obedience that we truly have something to say. The Bible teaches us about "casting down arguments and every high thing that exalts itself against the knowledge of God, bringing every thought into captivity to the obedience of Christ, and being ready to punish all disobedience when your obedience is fulfilled" (2 Cor. 10:5–6).

In the book *The Imitation of Christ*, Thomas à Kempis reflects on obedience and submission, saying,

> It is a very great thing to obey, to live under a superior and not to be one's own master, for it is much easier to be subject than it is to command. Many live in obedience more from necessity than from love. Such become discontented and dejected on the slightest pretext; they will never gain peace of mind unless they subject themselves wholeheartedly for the love of God.[20]

Second, an Attitude and Tone of Voice Make a Difference

The tendency to respond positively or negatively when expressing ourselves and knowing the power of positive vs. negative words make a significant difference. Tone of voice also matters; the spoken word and the impression it makes on everyone who hears us has an impact. Also, it is not about what one says but rather the way he or she says it. Case in point:

Both the priest Zacharias and the Virgin Mary were addressed by angel Gabriel. His initial words to both of them were "do not be afraid" to dispel their fear, then announced the good news! Both responded simply with the question: How could it be? Zacharias said, "How shall I know this? For I am an old man and my wife is well advanced in years." Mary said, "How could this be, since I do not know a man?" For Zacharias, the angel muted him and he became unable to speak for nine months and eight days until the naming of the child as the angel foretold. That is because he did not believe the angel's words. Meanwhile, Mary asked the question but did not doubt. That is why she said, "Behold the maidservant of the Lord. Let it be to me according to your word" (Luke 1:38).

The whole point is the contrast between the disbelieving question of Zacharias and the believing question of Mary.

Chapter Five

LOVING HIS BRIDE
NO MATTER HOW SHE LOOKS!

If you have seen the film *27 Dresses,* a classic romantic comedy starring Katherine Heigl as Jane, you might wonder why Jane cares about everyone else except herself. In the movie, she has been a bridesmaid at twenty-seven weddings yet never a bride. The movie is inspired by a true story. Two things about Jane: she never says no to her friends. Every time she selflessly plans her friends' weddings, always the bridesmaid but never the bride. However, her joy comes as she glances at the groom and see his face beaming with happiness. At one point in the movie, she explains her feelings: "'Cause his face says it all, you know! The pure love is there." She is not concerned about being unnoticed or sidelined as a bridesmaid.

That takes us to the scriptures. John the Baptist expresses his happiness and says, "He who has the bride is the bridegroom; but the friend of the bridegroom, who stands and hears him, rejoices greatly because of the bridegroom's voice. Therefore the joy of mine is fulfilled" (John 3:29). The bride here is the church. No doubt St. John's inspired picture of the groom is the work of the Holy Spirit. Throughout the Gospels, Jesus refers directly to himself as the bridegroom and uses a parable to teach about being the bridegroom, and the New Testament letters depict the church as the bride. John the Baptist may have not recognized the bridegroom revelation at first, but he encountered the living God in Jesus coming up from the water and saw the heavens part and the Spirit descend upon Him like a dove. Then a voice came up from heaven, "You are my beloved Son, in whom I am well pleased" (Mark 1:11).

John the Baptist understood then that his calling was to help the bride be as beautiful as she could be to meet her groom, all the while knowing that the bridegroom was going to love his bride no matter how she looked. St. Augustine says about the church, "We esteem her highly. She is worthy spouse of so great a Lord. The goodness of the Bridegroom in fact has been exceptional. He found a harlot and made her a virgin… The Church is there pure. May she remain pure, may she fear the seducer, may she be far from any who could defile her!"[21]

Not only that, the Church guards her purity but also persistently avoid calamities of comparing, complaining, and competing. A dispute arose among some of John's disciples and the Jews about purification. So they came to John and addressed him as rabbi. Then they complained about Jesus without referring to his name. They referred to Him as "He who was with you beyond the Jordan, to whom you have testified." They compared what they did and what Jesus was doing—"He is baptizing, and all are coming to Him!" Even though Jesus was not doing the work but His disciples were. If they had bothered to reflect on what John had said in witness concerning Jesus, they would not have been so upset and they would have been more respectful. Instead, they complained about what Jesus was doing as if it was something he should not do.

Notice that John's joy is complete and at peace, not envious or bitter, when he tells his disciples, "I am not the Christ for who comes from above is above all." John redirects his disciples to understand that Jesus is the one to follow. Jesus comes from heaven and, by his very nature, is greater than anything John could ever be. Then he affirms the fact that he was going to decrease his role so that Jesus would increase in the lives of his disciples and the world—that Jesus is the Son, and the Father loves the Son and has given all things into His hand. Then he called their attention to the fact that every gift comes from heaven. This truth is as relevant today in our churches as it was true then.

We all need to be firmly mindful of this fact. If we were, we could remove all causes of jealously and envy among members of the body of Christ. Who are we to compare and complain that someone else has gifts that we don't have or should have to be able to compete? After all, every good gift and every perfect gift is from above, coming down from the Father of lights, with whom there is no variation or shadow of turning (James 1:17).

Chapter Six

THE AMAZING APOSTLE

St. Thomas is truly an amazing apostle, according to the book *Ecclesiastical History* of Bishop Eusebius of Caesarea. Born in Galilee and died AD 53 in Madras, India. Thomas is one of the twelve apostles. The Gospel according to John reveals Thomas's character of devotion and enthusiasm to be with Jesus and to die with him. When Jesus planned to return to Judaea, the disciples warned him of the Jews wanting to stone him, to which Thomas replied, "Let us also go, that we may die with him" (John 11:16). At the Last Supper, Thomas could not understand what Jesus meant when he said, "I will come again and receive you to Myself; that where I am, there you may be also. And where I go you know, and the way you know" (John 14:3–4). Thomas said to Him, 'Lord, we do not know where you are going, and how can we know the way?'" Jesus answered, "I am the way, the truth, and the life" (John 14:5–6).

St. Thomas was surely an amazing man, for every adversity he may have brought to the assembled disciples has the seed of an equivalent or greater benefit. It was not mere chance when Lord Jesus came to the disciples while they were full of fear and anxiety. After the crucifixion, fearing the crowd would come after them, His disciples gathered together and shut the doors. Unexpected, He stood in their midst and said, "Peace be with you." It is also not a mere chance that He came when Thomas was not there. He wanted to establish an eternal reality and a new doctrine. But how did the Lord do it? He allowed Thomas to express his doubts for the sake of us all.

The unbelieving Thomas represents all the unbelievers all over the world when he said, "Unless I see in His hands the print of the nails, and put my finger in the prints of the nails, and put my hand into His side, I will not believe." It is not mere chance that the Lord came for the second time when the doors were shut and again stood in the midst and said, "Peace to you!" Notice He did not say to them, "peace be with you" but "peace to you" because now he has been with them before and breathed on them and said to them, "Receive the Holy Spirit." Dear brothers and sisters, the Holy Spirit dwells in the temple of your soul. The peace is within each one of us. Are we really peaceful? Do we communicate peace into our homes and with our families, neighbors, and all who cross our path?

It is not mere chance that St. Thomas saw the resurrected Lord standing in their midst while the doors were being shut, and the Lord knew Thomas's doubts and said to him, "Reach your finger here, and look at my hands; and reach your hand here, and put it in my side. Do not be unbelieving, but believing" (John 20:27).

Thomas answered, "My Lord and My God," hence declaring the most powerful and direct evidences for the doctrine of the deity of Christ, or the belief that Jesus is fully human and fully divine united in one.

Not only did we receive such belief that the Lord Jesus is our Lord and our God, but also we are blessed. That is, when Jesus said to Thomas, because you have seen me, you have believed—here is the punch line—"Blessed are those who have not seen and yet have believed" (John 20:29).

St. Thomas spent the following years spreading the good news. He evangelized Parthia (modern Khorasan), then extended his apostolate into India. He proclaimed that the Lord has risen and redeemed man from sin, that He was crucified on the cross for the redemption of human sins on behalf of all humanity. St. Thomas traveled many places proclaiming the resurrection of the Lord. *Ecclesiastical History* records his martyrdom as having occurred under the king of Mylapore at Madras (now Chennai), where Santhome Cathedral Basilica, his traditional burial place, is located. His relics, however, supposedly were taken to the west and eventually enshrined at Ortona, Italy.[22] It is our turn to do the same and show the world the joyous spirit of our salvation. Give hope to the hopeless, counsel the doubtful, comfort the sorrowful, forgive the injuries, bear wrongs patiently, and pray for the living and dead.

Chapter Seven

THE LIGHT OF THE WORLD

I have come as light into the world, that whoever
believes in Me should not abide in darkness.
—John 12:46

During World War II, a newsman named Clarence W. Hall followed
American troops through Okinawa, the largest island in a group of
islands southwest of Japan. Okinawa was the scene of fierce combat between the Imperial Japanese Army and US Army and Marine
forces (April 1–June 21, 1945). During the campaign, Clarence and
his jeep driver came upon an Okinawan village that stood out as a
beautiful example of a Christian community! The entire village had
been transformed by the "Light of the world"—Jesus, the Christ!
    Clarence wrote,

> We had seen other Okinawan villages…down
> at the heels and despairing: by contrast, this one
> shone like a diamond in a dung heap. Everywhere
> we were greeted by smiles and dignified bows.
> Two little old men bowed low and began to
> speak. One says he's the mayor of the village, the
> other's the schoolmaster, the Bible the older one
> has in his hand…

"Proudly the two old men showed us their spotless homes, their
terraced fields…their storehouses and granaries, their prized sugar

mill." Clarence went on to say that he saw no jails and no drunkenness in the village. So the question is, How did it happen?

Clarence was told that an American missionary had come to the village some thirty years earlier. While there, he had led two elderly villagers to Jesus and left them with a Japanese translation of the Holy Bible. These two new believers studied the Holy Scriptures and started leading their fellow villagers to Jesus! The jeep driver said that he was amazed at the difference between this village and the villages around it. As reported by Rev. George R. Dillahunty, he remarked, "So this is what comes out of only a Bible and a couple of old guys who wanted to live like Jesus."

That is exactly how the light of the world (Matt. 5:14) can transform each one of us. Shining through us, His light can make us a supernova. It has been said a supernova releases incomprehensible power in a brief flash and can burn brighter than billions of suns. Thus, we should never underestimate the powerful transformation of His light and what it can do through us. One holy person can save not only his family or community but also a city, a nation. That is what happened with one missionary in Okinawa, Japan, more than a century ago. From this day on, let's not underestimate what we can do when clothed with humility and sustained by His grace. Let's not be tempted to say, "'I am just a small candle, not a supernova. I can't save a city or a nation!'"[23]

True enough, but God can! He can make us a supernova and do great wonders...if only we surrender to Him. We have seen in this true story what He did with a single American missionary in a small Okinawan village. But there is no need to go far to spread his word. Look at what the Lord did with the scared, secluded disciples who thought they were seeing a ghost, and with the two disciples on the road to Emmaus. They'd lost hope and were convinced that the Master was dead like any other man. Once He appeared and met with them and they received the Holy Spirit, they boldly preached, witnessed, and gladly gave their lives proclaiming the good news. By embracing the Holy Spirit, there is no reason for any of us to remain in darkness or refrain from proclaiming the good news as well!

St. Augustine says,

John writes: "God is light and in him is no darkness at all." [1 John 1:5] Although he is speaking of light, the words are obscure. The sun is also light, the moon is also light, a lamp is also light. There must be in God something very greatly superior to these lights in grandeur, in brightness, in quality... Perhaps we shall approach it if we do all we can to be illuminated by it.[24]

Chapter Eight

QUALITIES OF DIVINE NATURE

Such knowledge is too wonderful for me; it is high, I cannot attain it.
—Psalm 139:6

Surely it takes an unwavering commitment to invest in one's character. It is not about treading the path of perfection but rather a constantly renewed pursuit of excellence. It is all about human connection and how we treat one another, reflecting on what presumably ought to be the gentleness of the human soul.

Love, do good, bless, and pray! Four key directives set the standard for connection, communication, and dealing with another human being. When the Lord says, "Love your enemy" (Luke 6:27), the Greek word used for love—*agape*—does not mean romantic love, liking someone, or even friendship. Agape love is the divine love of the Lord toward his Son, Jesus Christ. It is the type of love that God commanded all his faithful children to have for everyone regardless of their religion, color, race, ethnicity, sex, or sex characteristics. Such divine love is not based on one's feelings; rather it is a set of behaviors, responses, and actions. So when we are commanded to love our enemy, it means that we can show kindness, compassion, and benevolence regardless of the feelings we may have at the time.

In other words, the believer is commanded to have unreserved, unconditional desire for the well-being of our fellow man. That happens when love and respect replace hatred and injustice. The believer should not expect to receive anything in return and/or be compensated for his good deeds and charity to those in need. Everyone values this kind of love. This applies equally to those whose behavior you do not like, even when taking a stand and opposing their views and thus speaking against them. But if you have agape love for your enemies, in humility you can express your dislike and opposition accompanied by a total desire for their well-being.

The Lord Jesus shows us how to enact this agape love for our enemies. First, even for those who hate you, you must wish them well and to treat them rightly, truly, and justly. Second, bless those who curse you; speak well of them, praise them, and give comfort to them. Lastly, pray for the means to lift them up, appealing to God on their behalf.

Sadly, Luke 6:29—"To whom who strikes you on the one cheek, offer the other also. And from him who takes your cloak, do not withhold your tunic either"—is often explained incorrectly. Regretfully, a common misunderstanding of this verse has brought untold misery to many people.

Christian parents have been telling their children to turn the other cheek in school and allow others to take advantage of and abuse them. Similarly, wives have suffered degradation and abuse due to ignorance or negligence of their spouses. The Lord Jesus is not saying to the wives and children to be doormats and passively accept abuse. In fact, He is teaching us a way to passively resist abuse by others, especially within the family. To stand still and offer the left cheek actually becomes an act of resistance. The abuser's powerlessness is exposed for all to see; should he try again, he would be shamed and dishonored for his cruelty. Similarly, if anyone would take away your coat, this would be robbery. In giving away the "tunic," which is an inner garment, it would leave you naked. The aggressor might be embarrassed.

Understanding Luke 6:29 properly, what is really being exposed is the injustice. Giving your inner tunic as well as your coat exposes the injustice of having your coat taken in the first place. These two examples demonstrate how to "agape love" your enemies. They are powerful nonviolent ways to expose injustice.

These verses further expand the teaching to love our enemies by expecting nothing in return, which is a core Christian theme. The only way to win the battle of human frailty and aim for the well-being of whoever crosses our path is by agape love through doing good, blessing, and praying for all who inflect hardships on us.

St. Gregory of Nyssa provides a good analogy that reflects on the discrepancy between our human nature formed in God's likeness and some of the animal qualities we inherited that came into this world before we did. Thus, he says,

> These qualities have found their way into the human condition from the animal creation. But the likeness of God is not revealed by fighting spirit in the human race. The supreme nature is not characterized by the pleasure of procreation, or by cowardice, greed, or dislike of inferiority. These passions are very far from being marks of divinity.[25]

Chapter Nine

PROVE YOUR FAITH

What Is Faith?

Faith is the theological virtue by which we believe all what God says and reveals to us and all what the Holy Church proposes for our belief. St. Theodoret elaborates on faith, saying, "Faith requires knowledge, but in its turn knowledge has need of faith. As there cannot be faith without knowledge, so there cannot be knowledge without faith. Faith comes before knowledge: knowledge is subsequent to faith... Therefore: first of all, one must believe, then learn."[26]

In the Gospel according to Matthew, Jesus performed a unique miracle. "One was brought to Him who was demon-possessed, blind and mute; and He healed him, so the blind and mute man both spoke and saw. And all the multitudes were amazed and said, 'Could this be the Son of David?'" (Matt. 12:22–23). What questionable faith! They did not marvel and say, "We believe!" Even worse was the Pharisees' denial of faith when they said, "This *fellow* does not cast out demons except by Beelzebub, the ruler of the demons" (Matt. 12:24).

What about our faith? Do we believe all what God says? Does it show when our faith is confronted or tested with fire? Let us then reflect on how our Church Fathers were undaunted by threat to deny their faith.

When Polycarp (AD 69–155), a bishop of Smyrna, was asked by Roman authorities to curse Christ if he wanted to be released, he said, "Eighty and six years I have served Him, and He has done me no wrong." Polycarp went on to say, "How then can I blaspheme my

King and Savior? You threaten me with a fire that burns for a season, and after a little while is quenched; but you are ignorant of the fire of everlasting punishment that is prepared for the wicked." Polycarp was burned at the stake and pierced with a spear for refusing to burn incense to the Roman emperor. On his farewell, he said, "I bless you, Father, for judging me worthy of this hour, so that in the company of the martyrs I may share the cup of Christ."[27]

Centuries earlier, when three young men named Shadrach, Meshach, and Abednego faced a similar threat, they answered, "O Nebuchadnezzar…our God whom we serve is able to deliver us from the burning fiery furnace, and He will deliver us from your hand, O king. But if not, let it be known to you, O king, that we do not serve your gods" (Dan. 3:16–18). A similar experience but two different outcomes. Polycarp was burned alive, but Shadrach, Meshach, and Abednego left the furnace unharmed, in fact unsinged.

Two different results but the same display of faith. These men showed us that faith in God is not simply faith in what God can do. It's the belief that God is God whether He delivers us or not. He has the final say. And it is our decision to choose to follow Him through it all.

St. Ambrose says in this regard:

> Prove your faith by your trust, "Look at the birds of the air," says Jesus (Luke 12:24) What a splendid example for our faith to follow! If God's providence bestows an unfailing supply of food on the birds of the air who neither sow nor reap, we ought to realize that the reason for people's supply running short is human greed… Surely we should be all the more ready to believe that human beings, if they entrust themselves completely to God and free themselves of all their worries, will not lack anything.[28]

Chapter Ten

HEALTHY ATTRIBUTES DESPITE INFIRMITY

The healing of a paralytic at Bethesda is one of the many miracles of Jesus. It is the story of a man who suffered from debilitating illness for thirty-eight long years. When Jesus saw him lying there and knew he had been in that condition a long time, He said to him, "Do you want to be made well? (John 5:6).

That seems like a puzzling question. Who would not want to be healed? The Lord knows the man is crippled and has been suffering a long time, so why question him? The Bible says that a great multitude of sick, blind, lame, and paralyzed people were "waiting for the movement of the water" at the healing pools of Bethesda (John 5:3).

We discover amazing attributes and rare qualities in the man of Bethesda. Most likely this man, despite his paralysis, possessed healthy, unique attributes. Let us reflect on these.

He was a broken man, yet he did not react normally to the Lord's question. Were he an *assertive* man, he would say, "Yes! Sure!" Were he an *aggressive* man, he would have answered, "Is this a question to even ask? Why do you think I am here?" (Remember, the crippled man did not know who Jesus was.) Were he a *passive* man, he would have looked at Jesus and not even uttered a word, perhaps even turned his face way. Finally, were he a *passive-aggressive* man, he would have said, "Nice of you to ask. What can you do?" The man, however, answered simply and in brokenness "Sir, I have no man to put me into the pool" (John 5:7). In other words, he was alone and had no one to help him.

This man was also a gentle communicator—he did not complain and grumble about these selfish people who were taking advantage of his limitations, for every time he wants to enter the pool, another steps down before him. He just communicates to Jesus what happens, simply and objectively.

This man was also strong-willed and determined. No matter how long he needed to stay there or how many preceded him and were healed, he would not leave until he was made well. His strong will is also coupled with patience, and who could be that patient? Thirty-eight long years he spent there. Even before the birth of Jesus he was lying there, and despite it all, he did not give up and did not leave the place.

According to St. John Chrysostom, Jesus singled out the man who had waited for so many years in order to teach us to have perseverance. Imagine how, for all those years, the paralyzed man saw people come and go. They came with an ailment or sickness, then left healthy to enjoy life. The lame man stood his ground, accepted his ailment, and remained adamant to bear the weight of suffering, uncomplaining and unwilling to compare himself to others or reveal his disappointment as others made it to recovery.

He was surely a hopeful man—for all those years, he waited and waited until that one day, yes one day, he would make it and walk again healthy and strong. What gave him that hope? Seeing the power of God at work restoring people's health, though he did not see the angel of the Lord go down to stir up the water. Therefore, he remained hopeful that one day he, too, would be healed. It did not matter to him how long it would take; through the years he lived with unfading hope.

One might wonder about Christian people who are living in a world of instant gratification today. Would they have this kind of patience or hope? We surely find ourselves marveling at this man. After all that time, he wants to be healed. Moreover, he was still waiting and wanting for someone to do for him what he couldn't do for himself. No wonder, he readily consented that Jesus heals him once asked.

Though the man at Bethesda had these wonderful attributes—remarkable attributes from behavioral sciences point of view—they did not restore him. Such attributes might result in worldly success, but wonderful attributes alone are not an answer to free man from sin. The lame man suffered from spiritual infirmity caused by sin. That is why when Jesus found him in the temple, He said to him, "See, you have been made well. Sin no more, lest a worse thing come upon you" (John 5:14).

Whatever healthy attributes one may have to serve him well in life, it will not cure him from the paralysis of sin. The sanctity and liberation from sin will only happen if there is true penance, for "if we confess our sins, He is faithful and just to forgive our sins and cleanse us from all unrighteousness" (1 John 1:9).

In this regard, St. Cyril of Jerusalem enlightens us with these words:

> It is not the body that sins, but the soul. The body is only an instrument; it is like the outward clothing of the soul. It becomes impure if it is used for fornication, but it becomes the temple of the Holy Spirit if it is united to his sanctity. These are not my words. The Apostle Paul says them: 'Do you not know that the body is the temple of the Holy Spirit within you?'[29]

Chapter Eleven

PROCLAIMING THE GOOD NEWS

He who hears you hears Me, he who rejects you rejects Me,
and he who rejects Me rejects Him who sent Me.
—Luke 10:16

Proclaiming the good news of God in Christ through word and deed is what the Lord Jesus expects His followers to do. It ought to be a mission for every believer, for the Bible tells us "And every day in the temple and at home they did not cease to teach and proclaim Jesus as the Messiah" (Act 5:42). It is true that sharing one's faith with a nonbeliever can be a daunting and difficult task for many, but it is also incredibly rewarding. Evangelism is the cornerstone of the Christian faith, but few are willing to engage in this great mission. It is easy to envision a priest in the pulpit preaching the word of God to members of the congregation. But through our baptismal covenant, we all are called to proclaim the good news. Many believers think it is just the priest's job in the church till the day we see what we had not expected—even the priest does it away from the pulpit.

In the early 1970s, St. George Coptic Church in Philadelphia has its first priest ever. He was a righteous man, a well-published theologian, and a humble priest. Members of the congregation frequently saw him dressed in his priestly robe handing out small pictures and pamphlets to pedestrians in front of the city hall in downtown Philadelphia. Those who saw him assumed that he was seeking charity or begging for money. The congregation at the time consisted of a small number of families. Members of the church felt confused, indignant, and resentful at the thought of their priest begging and/ or acting in a dishonorable manner. Little did they know that he was living out the story of Christ in him, inside the church and out.

When some members discreetly approached the righteous and humble priest regarding the matter, they discovered this saintly man was on a mission to evangelize. He actually smiled and said: "How will they hear? It is our responsibility to deliver the good news. Preaching and teaching are not acts to be confined within the walls of the church or limited to church members. We all must show Christ through our daily lives and work and be prepared to give reasons for the hope within us." He added that we can do that by talking about our faith with neighbors and others. He asked his congregation to do the same and invited others to come to the church where Christ is proclaimed. His charitable deed not only was a great lesson but a humbling and unforgettable experience for those who met with him.

How can we evangelize? No matter how hard it seems to undertake this responsibility of making others believe in Jesus, if we earnestly pray and ask for God's grace, it will be done. We surely need to study the Bible and devote ourselves to reading it daily. We also should spend fifteen minutes alone with the Lord in daily meditation, mindful how His presence is vital for growing in the faith. St. Isaac of Nineveh says, "Be mindful of God, so that in every moment he may be mindful of you, he will give you salvation."[30]

Such a brief time with the Lord helps prevent us from constantly being on the move. We are always going, doing, and overly busy, and with that comes stress, anxiety overlooking our first priority in life. The faithful, whether in school, at work, or at home, should know the importance of these devotional times for growing in the faith. St. Isaac exhorts, "Do not forget him, letting yourselves be seduced by vain distraction. Do you want him to forget you in your time of temptation?... Remain constantly before his face, think of him, remember him in your heart. Otherwise, if you only meet him from time to time, you risk losing your close friendship with him."[31] Such intimate relations with the Lord will empower the faithful to evangelize and will bear fruit.

Proclaiming the message of salvation can be *peacefully and cheerfully* promulgated to others face-to-face, or it can be done on the internet reaching out to friends, peers, and strangers alike. My mind often flashes back to the zeal of our righteous priest and his enthusiasm in proclaiming the faith to strangers passing by in downtown Philadelphia. It was all part of his devotional life and his profound love for the Lord and His people. Words from scripture still flash through my mind: "How then shall they call on Him in whom they have not believed? And how shall they believe in him whom they have not heard? And how shall they hear without a preacher" (Rom. 10:14)?

Evangelizing must also be done *fearlessly and boldly* when we proclaim the good news to others. The Lord said, "Behold I give you the authority to trample over serpents and scorpions. And all the power of the enemy and nothing by any means shall hurt you" (Luke 10:19). During the 2011 uprising in Egypt, millions witnessed on TV a new Christian convert from Islam filled with passion calling on others to adopt his newly found "true" faith. He stood in the midst of a subway station proclaiming the good news of salvation and how Jesus Christ is the Savior of the world. He was shouting, "I was blind and now I see," giving glory to God.

Lovingly and kindly is another important approach when proclaiming the salvation message. The rewards are heavenly, for the Lord says, "Rejoice because your names are written in heaven" (Luke 10:20). We are to love not only our neighbors but all members of the human race who cross our path and wish for them to know Christ and be saved. One is reminded of Moses. He loved his people, his brothers, and his sisters so much that he asked to be blotted out of the book of life if the people did not receive forgiveness of their sins (Exod. 32:32). That is how much we ought to love and care about people in our lives.

Finally, everywhere we go, we must always proclaim the good news. As faithful Christians, we must serve as a model to emulate, for deeds speak louder than words.

Chapter Twelve

LORD, IF YOU HAD BEEN HERE!

The Lord Jesus delayed visiting Lazarus for two days when he was sick, knowing that Lazarus would die. Though both of his sisters, Martha and Mary, sent for the Lord and He could have healed Lazarus, He did not. He told His disciple that He was glad He was not there. Jesus anticipated raising Lazarus from the dead as a sign to His disciples that they should believe (John 11:11–15). Once the Lord arrived in Bethany and met with Martha, she said to Him, "Lord, if you had been here, my brother would not have died" (John 11:21). When Mary came and saw Jesus, she fell down at His feet, weeping and repeating Martha's words in gentle reproach. "Therefore, when Jesus saw her weeping, and the Jews who came with her weeping, He groaned in the spirit and was troubled" (John 11:33).

Although the apostle John does not tell us specifically why Jesus wept, we can infer that the Lord grieved over death as a result of mankind's sin. The apostle Paul confirmed the correlation between sin and death: "Therefore, just as through one man sin entered the world, and death through sin, and thus death spread to all men" (Rom. 5:12). Groaning means to utter a deep moan indicative of pain or grief. Jesus groans and is troubled for our pain and loss. Having compassion for the weeping crowd, He wept. But Jesus did not stop there; He acted to relieve the pain and sadness and turn it to joy. He raised Lazarus from the dead.

Jesus has compassion for each one of us and feels our pain and sadness. He will raise us out of every deadly encounter and deadly sin even if we have been buried in it for some time and even when those around us feel hopeless and helpless. When Jesus wanted to raise Lazarus from the dead, He said, "Take away the stone," but Martha, who had witnessed the power of Jesus, did not believe what He was about to do. She said, "Lord, by this time there is a stench, for he has been dead four days" (11:39). Jesus said to her, "Did I not say to you that if you would believe you would see the glory of God?" Martha, who expressed her "belief knowledge" repeatedly, never envisioned that the Lord was going to raise Lazarus from the dead until "the last day"—but He did then and there, resurrecting her brother from death as He said He would.

Thus, the Lord Jesus performed the most powerful miracle of all. Not only that, but He taught Martha, Mary, and the rest of His disciples to have faith in Him beyond the state of "belief knowledge," and they were transformed to the "living faith" as they saw Lazarus, who had been dead for four days, come back to life. The crux of the matter is that Jesus groans today for our lack of faith as well when we say: "Could not Jesus perform this miracle for me?" As some have said, "Could not this man, who opened the eyes of the blind, also have kept this man from dying?" We, too, have to remain not only knowledgeable of what the Lord can do but have the true living faith that He will do for us what He promises.

Once in a while we hear and read about people who reveal unshakable faith in God even when they are subjected to deadly disaster. Former president George H. W. Bush visited Honduras soon after Hurricane Mitch had devastated that nation in 1998. Television interviewer Larry King asked Bush if natural disasters like this one shook his belief in God. The former president replied by telling of a seventy-three-year-old man who had lost all he owned. Through his tears, the man told Bush with confidence, "Every possession I had is gone, but...I have faith in God."

It is a powerful lesson to all of us when the Lord puts a promise in our heart. We have to believe it is going to happen so strongly, and nothing can pull us away from complete confidence that God is still in control. For God is omnipotent, omniscient, and omnipresent.

St. Clement of Alexandria points us to the importance of scholarship to ripen our faith when he says, "It is possible to be faithful Christian without knowing how to read. But it is impossible to understand the doctrine of the faith without having studied it. Accepting the right ideas, rejecting erroneous theses: this cannot be done by simple faith, but only by faith that has been ripened by scholarship."[32]

Chapter Thirteen

LIVING FAITH VERSUS PRACTICAL ATHEISM

A wonderful couple, Zacharias the priest and his wife, Elizabeth, were both righteous before God, walking blameless in all the commandments and ordinances of the Lord (Luke 1:5–6). Although they both had prayed for a long time, they had no child because Elizabeth was barren, and both were well advanced in years. It seemed that they had given up on the idea of becoming parents because to human reasoning it is impossible. Yet the word "impossible" is not to be found in God's plan.

One day, the angel of the Lord delivered the good news to Zacharias while he was serving as a temple priest offering incense in worship. The angel said to him, "Your prayer is heard; and your wife Elizabeth will bear you a son, and you shall call his name John. And you will have joy and gladness, and many will rejoice at his birth. He will be great in the sight of the Lord, and shall drink neither wine nor strong drink. He will also be filled with the Holy Spirit, even from his mother's womb" (Luke 1: 13–15).

Then came Zacharias's doubtful response to the angel, "How shall I know this? For I am an old man and my wife is well advanced in years" (Luke 1:18). In other words, he didn't believe the angel of the Lord, whose answer was swift and punitive: "I am Gabriel, who stands in the presence of God, and was sent to you and to bring you these glad tidings. But behold, you will be mute and not able to speak until the day these things take place, because you did not believe my words which will be fulfilled in their own time" (Luke 1:19–20). Zacharias was punished for his unbelief, though the Bible described both him and his wife as righteous and blameless. We have to wonder sometimes how God feels when we disappoint Him and doubt His promises due to our lack of faith.

In Matthew's Gospel (Matt. 8:5–11), there is a perfect picture of a true faith and how to live the faith. It is the story of the centurion who appeared before the majesty of the Lord for one purpose—to intercede and to plead on behalf of his servant. He did not tell our Lord what he needed or what he wanted him to do; he simply stated the problem. He says, "Lord, my servant is lying at home paralyzed, dreadfully tormented."

Jesus said to him, "I will come and heal him." The centurion answered and said, "Lord, I am not worthy that You should come under my roof. But only speak a word, and my servant will be healed." Then he gave the analogy of being a man under authority having soldiers under *his* authority who he tells what to do and they do it. When Jesus heard it, He marveled, and said to those who followed, "Assuredly, I say to you, I have not found such great faith, not even in Israel!"

Jesus wanted to make this evangelizing statement known to every one of us by having incorporated in the Gospel, to be remembered generation after generation. The centurion's statement in Matthew 8:8 became part of Christian tradition and the very words we say before partaking communion: "Lord, I am not worthy that you should enter under my roof, but only say the word and my soul shall be healed."

For our own self-searching, we may wonder whether our faith resembles the centurion's, placing our concerns, difficulties, and challenges before the Lord. Have we trusted Him with the solution whenever and however He plans it? Or are we like Zacharias, despite his righteousness, questioning the validity of the Lord's plan and His timing?

To help all of us rediscover and renew our faith in the great gift of God, we ought to remember what leaders of the church recently pointed out—the particularly dangerous phenomenon that faith has diminished in our time. And this dangerous phenomenon is called "practical atheism." Practical atheism basically refers to people who do not deny the truth of our faith, nor do they deny our religious rights, but they consider it merely irrelevant to daily life. They are detached from living a life of faith outside the practice of worship or attending church services. They are totally detached from being ambassadors and witnesses to our faith once they leave the church.

Practical atheism also refers to people who often believe in God in a superficial manner. They live as though God did not exist. Such a way of life is destructive, because it leads to a state of indifference to faith and indifference to the question of God. One cannot help but to recall the scripture in Revelation 3:16: "So then, because you are lukewarm, neither hot nor cold, I will spew you out of my mouth." In this state of indifference, the faithful do not attempt to provide the nourishment of faith outside the church. No encounter of Jesus outside the mass. No encounter with the needy, the poor, and the sick. No encounter with those who are suffering. No witnessing of our faith or proclaiming the good news of our Lord Jesus the Redeemer.

The priest's role is to help all of us be on fire in the faith. Our role is to get people outside the life of Holy Communion who do not attend mass or go to church to resurrect their fire in the faith with the help of God.

Many people today have a limited idea of Christian faith because they identify it with a mere system of beliefs and values rather than the truth of God. God was anxious to communicate with human beings in a relationship of love with them. In fact, the root of every Christian doctrine and every Christian value is the meeting of man and God in Jesus Christ.[33]

Chapter Fourteen

EXODUS: THE MAIN IMPACT OF GENOCIDAL ACTS AGAINST CHRISTIANS

Persecution of Christians is modern-day 'genocide'
—Sec. Jeremy Hunt

In the Gospel according to St. Luke, Jesus sends the seventy out "as lambs among wolves." They are instructed to "carry neither money bags, sack, nor sandals; and greet no one along the road" (Luke 10:4). He calls on them to take the risk of going to foreign lands without many necessary things. They have their mission to heal the sick and proclaim "the kingdom of God has come near to you." They are to eat what is set before them. They are to risk rejection by their hosts who do not receive them. Without carrying necessities for their own survival, they must convey a new message to a cynical and hostile world, vulnerable among wolves as they preach the Gospel. They obviously were setting out into dangerous and risky territory, yet they had to be peaceful, "wise as serpents and harmless as doves" (Matt. 10:16).

St. Augustine saw this as an analogy in which Jesus was calling Christians to offer their whole body to persecutors rather than their head, as serpents do (they curl up their body around their head to protect it). This is emphasized by pairing the commandment to be like serpents with a commandment to be like doves.[34] Both the snake-shrewdness and the dove-harmlessness are designed to keep the sheep out of trouble.

Jesus does not mean for us to get into as much difficulty as possible. He means: risk your lives as vulnerable, noncombative, sheeplike, courageous witnesses, but try to find ways to give witness in a manner that avoids unnecessary persecution. During their mission, the disciples learn the lesson of facing dangers while rejoicing and said, "Lord, even the demons are subject to us because of Your name" (Luke 10:17).

They have come to trust in God and the power of Jesus's name. They realize that their success is due to the name of Jesus they invoke with faith; it rather than their own power is what terrorizes demons. When the disciples learn of Jesus, now He tells them not to rejoice because "the spirits are subject to them" but to rejoice "because their names are written in heaven" (Luke 10:20). Their names are written in heaven because, by being lambs in the midst of wolves, they have learned their need for God and they have grown to carry their mission in a spirit of humility, docility, and as a lamb, easy to handle and easily led by the Good Shepherd. Risking our lives in a hostile world for being faithful to Jesus Christ is truly worth the risk. When Jesus reminds us that He sends us just as the Father has sent Him (John 20:21), He spoke as one who has been sent as the Lamb of God in the midst of wolves.

By becoming a man born of the Virgin Mary, Jesus's life was one of constant threats and dangers from several "wolves." It started with King Herod, who tried to kill Him even when He was still a child. The Pharisees plotted His death after He spoke and performed miracles. And even one of His close disciples, Judas, decided to betray Him after all the love that Jesus had shown him. It behooves us to follow the master, Jesus the Lamb of God, who is the perfect and the ultimate sacrifice for our sins. We ought to remember what He said to us, "'A servant is not greater than his master.' If they persecuted Me, they will persecute you. If they kept My word, they will keep yours also" (John 15:20).

Generation after generation since Christ till end of times, there will be always two distinct groups—the good and the evil. The good are the ones who are least, humble, and poor in spirit who love the Lord and delight in the good news of their Savior and want to serve and proclaim the salvation massage. The evil are the mighty rulers who possess wealth, power, and authority yet hate the name of Christ and Christians. They persecute the Christians where they find them and drive them away from their own land. There will be others, too, who hate themselves, society, harmony, and peace on earth. Time and time again, similar to what happened in Bethlehem, we will hear lamentation, weeping, and great mourning, like, "Rachel weeping for her children, refusing to be comforted, because they were no more" (Matt. 2:18).

Jesus calls us to go out into the world as lambs among wolves. We encounter this same crucified but living Lamb of God in the Eucharistic celebration. He is the one and only Good Shepherd who walks with His flock always. Tragedies strike and the innocent everywhere are massacred. Bloodshed, persecution, discrimination, and imprisonment of the innocent will be with us as part of our Christian history as long as there is life on earth. According to BBC News, in 2019, Christians were the most persecuted religious group. The BBC reported that the main impact of "genocidal acts against Christians is exodus" and that Christianity faced being "wiped out" from parts of the Middle East.[35]

However, even when facing dangers, taking risks, or losing lives out of love for the Lord Jesus no matter what it costs us, we will grow in the sense of our need for Him. We shall depend on Him with faith and trust, and our love and desire for Him will grow so much more than we desire Him now. By so doing, we shall walk in the footsteps of our Lord and be like Jesus, the Lamb of God, here on earth. It is then and only then that we shall truly thrive and rejoice, because our names, too, will be written in the book of life.

As written in *The Imitation of Christ*, The Disciple states,

O Lord, I shall suffer willingly for Your sake whatever You wish to send me. I am ready to accept from Your hand both good and evil alike, the sweet and the bitter together, sorrow with

joy; and for all that happens to me I am grateful.
Keep me from all sin and I will fear neither death
nor hell. Do not cast me out for ever nor blot me
out of the Book of Life, and whatever tribulation
befalls will not harm me.[36]

Chapter Fifteen

GOD'S LONGING FOR YOU

O Lord, You searched me and known me, You know my sitting down and my rising up; You understand my thought afar off.
—Psalm 139:1–2

For years, we heard and read empowering messages to pursue God, and there is certainly an important desire to encounter Him in more intimate ways and to welcome Him in our lives. But as we study the scriptures and the Lord opens our minds and hearts, we discover the Lord Jesus is always the one who initiates love—it is our role to respond. Only in the Bible do we find majestic and beautiful portraits of God's longing for man. It is His call that grows out again and again that echoes in the human heart, transcends the words we read in the scriptures, and continually touches us and draws the human heart. We are God's first love, and He wants to be our first love as well and have an intimate personal relationship with us. "God is faithful, by whom you were called into fellowship with his Son Jesus Christ our Lord" (1 Cor. 1:9).

God's original design for his creation was to have a relationship with the people He created, to dwell in their midst, manifesting His ever-shinning glory until all creation would be filled with the knowl-edge of His Glory. The apostle John briefly describes the nature of the relationship we are to have with God. "Behold what manner of love the Father has bestowed on us, that we should be called children of God. Beloved, now we are children of God; and it has not yet been revealed what we shall be, but we know that when He is revealed, we shall be like Him, for we shall see Him as He is. And everyone who has this hope in Him purifies himself, just as He is pure" (1 John 3:1–3).

The scriptures read:

> When they [the people] found him on the other side of the sea, they said to Him, "Rabbi, when did you get here?" Jesus answered, "Most assuredly, I say to you, you seek me, not because you saw the signs, but because you ate the loaves and were filled. Do not labor for food that perishes, but for food that endures to everlasting life, which the Son of Man will give you, because God the Father has set His seal on Him. (John 6:26–27)

Reflecting on this passage, let us pause with the question, *Why do we seek Jesus?*

Each one of us, myself included, seek for Jesus because of our wants and needs. Each one of us presents a list of demands and wants Him to answer our prayers sooner rather than later. His answer is usually framed in four categories: no, slow, grow, or go. One can imagine that the Lord says, "I will give you what you want, but that is not what I want!"

He wants us to seek Him, know Him, and love Him. To "seek first His kingdom and His righteousness, and all these things will be given to you as well" (Matt. 6:33). In Psalm 23, the first verse is, "The Lord is my shepherd; I shall not want." Personally, I admit that I frequently present my concerns and wants rather than seeking Him and being mindful of His presence in my life and trusting every want and concern to His care. What about concerns and big decisions that demand an immediate answer, some may ask? Pivotal concerns and decision-making should be navigated through prayer, reading scripture, and seeking the counsel of wise, trusted Christian people. Thus, trusting the Lord to guide one through to a safe harbor.

What did the multitude do and what can we do differently?

When Jesus was on earth, the multitude acted the same as we do today. They crowded Him because all were eager for something, eager to be healed or taught or fed. As He supplied their many wants and granted their requests, He was looking for one or two who would follow Him just to be near Him. Just to dwell in His presence. Let us comfort the Lord a while by letting Him know that we seek Him just to dwell in His presence, to be near Him. Not for teaching, not for material gain, not even for a message, but for Him and Him alone. Let us learn to sit at the feet of the Lord and be in His company as "Mary has chosen that good part, which will not be taken away from her" (Luke 10:42). Also, let us daily find quality time to tune our attention to hear His gentle knock at the door of our hearts and hear His words: "Behold, I stand at the door and knock. If anyone hears My voice and opens the door, I will come in to him, and dine with him and he with Me" (Rev. 3:20).

Finally, let us remember that the desire of the human heart to be loved is something learned from the Great Divine Heart. We were created for fellowship with Him. God has created us with that need and He can fill it. In *Confessions*, Augustine wrote, "You stir man to take pleasure in praising you, because you have made us for yourself, and our heart is restless until it rests in you."[37]

Chapter Sixteen

WHICH MASTER WILL YOU SERVE?

"No one can serve two masters; for either he will hate the one and love the other, or else he will be loyal to the one and despise the other."
—Matthew 6:24

"Which Master Will You Serve?" is the title of a homily presented by His Holiness Pope Tawadros II on the first Sunday of Lent, March 3, 2019. Known as the "the Treasures' Sunday," the Coptic pope added another title, "the Choices Sunday," which relates perfectly to the Lord's words in scripture. It speaks boldly to each believer as to the choice he or she will make. Which master will one serve? "God or mammon, for no one can serve two masters; for either he will hate the one and love the other, or else he will be loyal to the one and despise the other" (Matt. 6:24).

In this regard, St. Paul in his epistle to the Colossians says, "Set your mind on things above, not on things on the earth" (Col. 3:2). We need to make it a habit to structure our days during Lent and recognize our priorities. As such, we can learn to differentiate between the important stuff and the pedestrian stuff. Therefore, it is essential to take specific and practical steps to set our minds on things above before engaging in earthly activity. The words of Pope Tawadros II enlighten us and pave the way to set our minds on things above.

First, *daily devotion*. Spending time with the Lord is the initial step toward this goal. First and foremost, "Save your soul, for what profit is it to a man if he gains the whole world and loses his own soul?" The pope continues, "God has given us twenty-four hours a day. Could we devote few short moments to spend it with the Lord?" He added, "Shutting your door means shutting your mouth" and refraining from any type of digital media that disrupt your presence with the Lord.

"I sought the Lord and He heard me" (Ps. 34:4). About the prayers that are not heard, St. Augustin says,

> If someone has not been heard it means he has not sought the Lord… Seeking to obtain something from the Lord does not mean seeking the Lord himself… When you turn to God, do not seek some favor from him, Seek the Lord himself and he will hear you. He will interrupt your prayer saying: "Here I am. Yes, surely, here I am here. What do you want? What is your request? Everything I can give you is nothing in comparison to the gift of myself. Accept me, find your joy in me, talk with me. Touch me with the hands of your faith and you will be united with me."[38]

Second, *money as God's gift*. Pope Tawadros II reflects also on money and how it should not be a master. Many rich people use their wealth to establish projects and do great deeds not only to benefit the needy but also to build schools and hospitals that serve all. They offer wonderful charitable donations for many worthwhile purposes. This is unlike those who worship money as god—they are not rich; they are fools. Speaking of the parable of the rich fool in Luke 12:16–21, the pope depicts the futility of the belief that wealth can secure prosperity for good life or good health. There is a difference between whether wealth is a goal or a means. Wealth can be a source of many virtues, such as the virtue of thanksgiving, of satisfaction, of contentment, mercy, and stewardship.

St. Maximus the Confessor elaborates on things that God has bestowed on His people. He says, "Not one of the things God has put at our disposal is forbidden in Scriptures. The Bible limits its self to reproving excess and correcting what is unreasonable. For example, there is no need to avoid eating, having children, possessing wealth, and administering it with justice; only avoid gluttony, luxury, and so forth."[39]

Third, *the necessity of fasting.* To liberate our soul, maintain a tranquil heart, and cultivate a peaceful mind, we must rise above merely external worship that does not avail with God. Worship must be joined with internal sincerity and appropriate conduct in our daily life. Fasting and other ascetic acts do not necessarily indicate virtue. St. Augustine reminds us that even heretics fast! God will not see these actions if we mistreat others. Our inner thoughts, our words, even what's spoken to ourselves really matters. For it can hold the power to run our lives and dictate our choices.

No time is better than Lent to "be renewed in the spirit of your mind" (Eph. 4:23). Lent is the primary penitential season in the church's liturgical year, reflecting the forty days Jesus spent in fasting and prayers in the desert. The church unites herself each year to the mystery of Jesus in the desert who vanquished the tempter for us. Lent is the spring season to revitalize our spiritual life and to start anew and leave behind once and for all that which separates us from the Lord. This means we must choose to put off the old self, letting go of old habits, patterns, and sins, and take up the new, focusing our thoughts and heart on Christ's truths. For our life is hidden with Christ in God.

Fourth, *attainment of perfect freedom.* In acquiring patience in the fight against concupiscence, there is no better healing than the words in *The Imitation of Christ.*

> Therefore, My child, do not pursue your lusts, but turn away from your own will. "Seek thy pleasure in the Lord and He will give thee thy heart's desires." If you wish to be truly delighted and more abundantly comforted by Me, behold, in contempt of all worldly things and in the cutting off all base pleasures shall your blessing be, and great consolation shall be given you. Further, the more you withdraw yourself from any solace of creatures, the sweeter and stronger comfort will you find in Me.[40]

Chapter Seventeen

FACING SEDUCTIVE POWERS WITH A WINNING STRATEGY

Then Jesus was led up by the Spirit into the
wilderness to be tempted by the devil.
—Matthew 4:1

Fathers of the Church have pointed to three important seasons for the spiritual growth of the faithful; they are the Great Lent, Resurrection, and Advent. Today we will focus on the Lenten journey, which is considered to be the most blessed and profound spiritual period in the Coptic calendar. It is fasted for a total of fifty-five days, consisting of the Week of Preparation, the Holy Forty Days, Lazarus Saturday, and the Holy Pascha Week.

What ought we to do during Lent? The quick answer is fasting, prayers, and almsgiving, but this is only partially true, for that is only a means to an end. The purpose of Lent is conversion, a total conversion in which we have an intimate relationship with the Lord. It is to actualize our claim in the mass that "our hearts are with the Lord." In Proverbs 23:26, the Lord says, "My son, give me your heart, and let your eyes observe my ways."

To reach that level of spiritual growth, we must imitate what the Lord did in the wilderness. The Bible tells us that "Jesus was led up by the spirit into the wilderness to be tempted by the devil" (Matt. 4:1). So let us follow His footsteps there and learn how He handled temptation and how He dealt with Satan.

At the beginning of the Lord Jesus's ministry, there was a declaration of His divine nature. As declared in Matthew 3:16–17, He was baptized and heard the affirming words of His Father, "This is My beloved Son, in whom I am well pleased." But then things took a different turn along a harsh path. Immediately after His baptism by John (John 1:29) and just before the start of His public ministry, the Holy Spirit led Jesus to his temptation in the wilderness. Thankfully, Jesus's victory in the face of temptation provides a great example when we find ourselves facing the seductive powers of Satan.

From this mighty example, we need to uncover Satan's tactics to lure the Lord's sons and daughters away from the path of righteousness.

The first tactic is *lust of the flesh*. Being without food for forty days; Jesus must have been very hungry! Notice that the tempter caught Jesus at a time when He was tired and hungry. So Satan uses the same tactic with us. Waiting for those vulnerable moments, Satan lures us with the glare of seductive suggestion that offers pleasures, quick relief, and fulfillment of desires.

When facing such challenges, it is important to follow Jesus's example by quoting the scripture "Man shall not live by bread alone but by every word that proceeds from the mouth of God" (Matt. 4:4, Deut. 8:3). We need to depend on the Lord and His word to help us fulfill physical needs. Only when we read and memorize the word can we use it when under attack.

The second tactic is *pride*. Satan again challenges Jesus's identity, sets Him on the pinnacle of the temple, and tells Him to throw Himself down. Jesus responds again with the word: "It is written again, 'You shall not tempt the Lord your God'" (Matt. 4:7).

The third tactic is *lust for power*. The next temptation had Satan appealing to the lust of power by taking Jesus to a high mountain and showing Him the kingdoms of the world. Then Satan offered to give them to Him if Jesus would worship him (Matt. 4:8).

Jesus again responds quoting the scripture, but this time He sharply and adamantly says to him, "Away with you, Satan! For it is written, 'You shall worship the Lord your God, and Him only you shall serve'" (Matt. 4:10, Deut. 6:13).

The Good Lord has shown us the way. We have the same tools to overcome Satan and temptations in general. Let us always remember, Satan has been defeated! We even have authority and ability to repel Satan by the blood of the cross. However, we must never take him lightly, for spiritual warfare and our conflict with him is very real. "For we do not wrestle against flesh and blood, but against principalities, against powers, against the rulers of the darkness of this age, against spiritual hosts of wickedness in the heavenly places" (Eph. 6:12).

Jesus used the Word of God, prayer, and fasting, and so can we. Jesus was focused on God's plan, as we must be with our faith, trust, and obedience to His plan, "Above all, taking the shield of faith with which you will be able to quench all the fiery darts of the wicked one" (Eph. 6:16).

The faithful have to retain their confidence in the Lord, persisting with firm endurance to be heavenly rewarded, "Therefore do not cast away your confidence, which has great reward. For you have need of endurance, so that after you have done the will of God, you may receive the promise: 'For yet a little while, and He who is coming will come and will not tarry. Now the Just shall live by faith; but if anyone draws back, My soul has no pleasure in him.' But we are not of those who draw back to perdition, but of those who believe to the saving of the soul" (Heb. 10:35–39).

Chapter Eighteen

SPIRITUAL INDIFFERENCE

The opposite of faith is not heresy, it's indifference.
—Elie Wiesel

Indifference is the trait of lacking interest or enthusiasm in things. When you feel indifference for something, you neither like it nor dislike it. Indifference can be compared to apathy, which means "lack of concern." These attitudes may have very little consequence until it impacts our spiritual life. That is exactly what the Lord means when He says, "To what then shall I liken the men of this generation, and to what are they like? They are like children sitting in the market-place and calling to one another, saying: 'We have piped the flute for you, and you did not dance; we mourned to you, and you did not weep'" (Luke 7:32). If there is anything that stirs divine impatience, it is spiritual indifference among those who hear the Gospel. We need to challenge ourselves and reflect on our attitude to see if there is any indifference within our spiritual life, toward others, or more importantly toward God.

Indifference can happen when the inner voice of the Holy Spirit speaks to us but we do not hear or are too busy to respond. Eventually, the voice of the Spirit, the cry of the needy, the suffering of our neighbors, and ultimately our personal convictions weaken, then are dismissed.

Indifference is the attitude of the person who does not care and is not interested in anyone except himself, his needs, and pleasure. Do we want to be in that person's company?

Indifference is the servant or Sunday school teacher who comes to class unprepared uses the same curriculum year after year, repeating the same lesson, and never exploring new material and being creative in dealing with those whom he serves. Do you want to be in his class?

Indifference is the spouse who never cares or expresses affections, who can't be bothered saying, "I love you," who blames everyone else for his misery and self-centeredness. Do you want to be in that kind of relationship?

Pray for Healing and Restoration

Compare that to the passion of a caring and self-giving person who loves you, sacrifices for you, and is happy to be in your company. The passion of a teacher who comes well prepared to serve, who is a good communicator and caring. Or to the passion of a loving spouse who gives his all to his soul mate. You see it in the person who longs to come to church and spend intimate time with the Lord, to sing and pray and meditate in His presence. Or the person who is full of enthusiasm and serious about gathering with the Lord and doing his best to seek and save souls.

For those who experience the attitude of indifference, let us earnestly pray they be healed and restored. Let us fervently ask for the grace that ignites our spirit with His love to serve and love our neighbor and hear the cries of the needy. Let us cultivate such magnificent virtues and learn to meditate and emulate Jesus passionate journey and the sacrificial love that God has for this world. Such love is so deep that He sent His one and only Son to die on a cross so that whoever would believe in Him would not perish but have everlasting life.

The Lord Jesus Christ is not indifferent to you and me. His love for us is fiery, jealous, and wonderfully passionate. We must do whatever we can to not fall into or remain in spiritual indifference; otherwise, the Lord says, "So then because you are lukewarm, and neither cold nor hot, I will spew you out of my mouth" (Rev. 3:16).

Chapter Nineteen

PRESENTATION OF THE LORD

The feast of the presentation of our Lord in the temple that the church commemorates is an important day in the earthly life of our Lord Jesus Christ (Luke 2:22–39). According to the Gospel, Mary and Joseph took the infant Jesus to the temple in Jerusalem forty days after His birth to complete Mary's ritual purification after childbirth and to perform the redemption of the firstborn son, in obedience to the law of Moses (Lev. 12:2–8). The Gospel of Luke explicitly says that Joseph and Mary took the option provided for poor people (those who could not afford a lamb; Lev. 12:8), sacrificing "a pair of turtledoves, or two young pigeons" to the Lord as a purification sacrifice.

The Most Holy Virgin, the Mother of God, had no need of purification, since she had given birth to the source of purification and sanctity without defilement. However, she humbly fulfilled the requirement of the law. At that time, the righteous elder Simeon was living in Jerusalem. He was a holy man and was noted as a very intelligent scholar. Simeon spent much time studying the prophets of Israel. During his biblical translation of the prophesies, he hesitated over the translation of Isaiah 7:14 ("Behold, a virgin shall conceive...") and was going to correct it to "a woman" instead. However, it had been revealed to him he would not die until he had seen the Christ born of a virgin.

St. Simeon on that day was inspired to go to the temple at the very moment when the Most Holy Theotokos and St. Joseph had brought the infant Jesus to fulfill the law. The God-receiver Simeon took the child in his arms, and giving thanks to God, he spoke the words repeated by the church every evening at vespers, "Lord, now You are letting Your servant depart in peace, according to Your word; for my eyes have seen Your salvation which you have prepared before the face of all peoples, a light to bring revelation to the Gentiles, and the glory of Your people Israel" (Luke 2:29–32).

Also in the temple was Anna the Prophetess. She is intentionally mentioned by name—along with her father, Phanuel, as well as being of the tribe Asher—to signify her role in witnessing to the Redeemer in the temple. Having been married and lived with a husband seven years from her virginity; this woman was now a widow of about eighty-four years. Yet she did not depart from the temple but served God with fasting and prayers night and day. When she saw the Christ child, she praised God and spoke of Him to all who were awaiting the Messiah. According to an old Russian tradition, *Righteous Anna the Prophetess* is depicted on the icons of the presentation of the Lord behind the virgin holds a scroll that reads, "This Child has established Heaven and earth"

Finally, it is important for us Christians to not easily pass over such an important event quickly, missing the depth of the symbolism hidden in the story. We have really "seen the True Light, received the Holy Spirit, found the true faith" in this experience of the kingdom of God. The question we must all ask ourselves sincerely is: What are we like when going into this world after such an encounter with Jesus? We could at least do what Anna did—praise God and speak of our messiah to all who do not know Him and proclaim the good news as well!

Chapter Twenty

THE FASCINATION OF ILLUSORY FREEDOM

I say to you that likewise there will be more joy in heaven over one sinner who repents than over ninety-nine just persons who need no repentance.

—Luke 15:7

This is a story about a truly loving God who rejoices with the angels, and His desire to do is predicated upon repentance. The story of the prodigal son is one of the most touching and best known passages in the Bible. It has been called the "Gospel within the Gospel." We all know it and it is well understood. But it is Lent, the church presents this story for one purpose, which is conversion and repentance. The Lord Jesus has warned us "unless you repent you will all likewise perish" (Luke 13:3) But it is wonderful and consoling to see this compassionate, loving father eagerly watching for his son's anticipated return.

So the story is not only about the prodigal son—it is about all of us, myself included. The call for repentance is being heard again in the here and now. Similarly, the Lord greatly desires us to repent of our sins and return to Him. Many of us, especially in a culture that propagates behaving like the younger son, possess this foolish ambition to be independent. Such unwise ambition is at the root of the sinner persisting in his sin. A sinful state is a departure and distance from God. A sinful state is also a state of constant discontent (Luke

15:12–13). Hence this parable has been given to us so we avoid separation from the security and grace of living within the bosom of our Heavenly Father.

We live in a culture that instills individualism, independence, and freedom, but at what price, and what kind of independence and freedom? The son in this story learned the hard way that independence leads to a life of dissatisfaction and disappointment. The fascination of illusory freedom, the abandonment of the father's house, leads the son, after squandering his fortune, to a state of extreme misery, obliged to feed swine and, still worse, wanting to feed on the husks the pigs ate.

Only after he hit bottom did the son come to his senses and realize he had lost everything. His repentance and decision to declare himself guilty before his father, the journey back, the father's generous welcome; the father's joy—all these were the process of conversion. The father did something remarkable, and as the Bible puts it, "But when he was still a great way off, his father saw him and had compassion, and ran and fell on his neck and kissed him" (Luke 15:20). Then he called for the "best robe" to put it on him (a sign of position), a ring for his finger (a sign of authority), sandals on his feet (reserved only for freemen), and the festive banquet, all symbols of that new life.

The picture of the father receiving the son back into a loving relationship is a picture of how we should maintain a state of penance and reconciliation. It teaches us how we should respond to repentant sinners as well. "For all have sinned and fall short of the glory of God" (Rom. 3:23). We are included in that "all," and we must remember that "all our righteousness are like filthy rags" apart from Christ (Isa. 64:6). It is only by God's grace that we are saved. That is the core message of the parable of the prodigal son.

BOOK THREE

THE EFFECTS OF FAMILY VALUES ON *ENJOYABLE FAMILY LIFE*

Qualities of character inspire the choice of mission

Chapter One

THE FLIGHT INTO EGYPT A TRUE LOVE STORY

"Arise, take the young Child and His mother, flee to Egypt, and stay there until I bring you word."
—Matthew 2:13

The flight into Egypt is a true love story in which Joseph does everything he can to keep the baby Jesus and his mother safe. We all ought to examine this love story carefully and do whatever we can to emulate the Holy Family, especially in trusting God, obedience, and humility.

Let us take a moment and envision the looming danger that the Holy Family was exposed to. The tiny family is instructed by the angel to arise and leave immediately, fearing evil Herod seeking the young child to destroy Him. If this danger was not enough, Joseph was asked to take Jesus to Egypt, the land of bondage to Israel and cruel to the infants of Israel, yet it is to be a place of refuge for the Holy Child.

One of the worst plagues in this modern life is fear and insecurity. Many if not most of the people feel quite insecure about the future, the unknown, and hidden dangers. In fact, we fear for ourselves, our safety, and our well-being. We fear powerful people and crafty men who want to do us harm. In summary, many of us lead lives crippled by fear and insecurity.

Joseph: A Faithful, Obedient Man

The flight to Egypt was indeed a trial of the faith of Joseph and Mary. But their faith, being tried, was found firm. Joseph did not wait till morning; he rose at once and, with Mary and the child, started by night on the long journey, thus reversing the Exodus story of the Hebrew flight from Pharaoh. After all, Egypt was a land of refuge before it was a land of bondage, and now it has returned to its welcoming nature. Egypt had always been a natural asylum for refugees from Palestine. Jeroboam had found shelter there (1 Kings 11:40), and at a later date, Johanan the son of Kareah and his companions had fled from Nebuchadnezzar to Egypt (Jer. 43:5–7).

St. Joseph did not object to any part of the plan, nor did he show any hesitation, procrastination, or fear. After the wise men were gone and they all went to sleep, the angel of the Lord appeared to him in a dream and told him to get up and flee to Egypt. He did not even question the magnitude of this task that he was about to undertake that very night. He rose and began his trip to Egypt in faithful obedience to the Lord's command.

Joseph the Silent Man

Although Joseph did not question the angel, Zacharias did, and even St. Mary did when she asked angel Gabriel, "How can this be, since I do not know a man" (Luke 1:34)? St. Joseph did not utter a word, even though of all the places he had to travel to, it was Egypt.

St. Joseph could have simply asked the angel, "Why Egypt?" This was, after all, an ironic choice given the circumstances. In the Genesis story, Egypt was the place of danger from which the Hebrews fled. Now it became a sanctuary for Jesus and his parents. Egypt was the place where Pharaoh ordered the midwives to murder male Hebrew babies, and so Joseph could find himself fleeing from Herod to face another danger in Egypt. But Joseph remained silent and in humility carried out the command.

Mary: the Handmaid of the Lord

What about St. Mary in this love story? She found herself awakened in middle of the night to start a long and exhausting trip. She did not say, could we wait until the morning? Or why do you listen or act on a dream? Or why must I disturb the child in the middle of His sleep? In the Gospel written by Luke, Mary was a model of what a follower of Jesus ought to be: she had faith in God, she thought deeply about what was happening to her, and she cooperated with God, holding nothing back. She was also a very human figure, experiencing distress and joy as she watched over her child. It is a story of love when the couple cooperated humbly with God's plan without a single question. Not only it is a love story, it is also an amazing display of faith in the Lord.

God's Concealed Plan

Our Lord is compassionate and merciful. God loves, God helps, God fights, and God wins. He plans our lives, though He may not reveal His plan to us out of protection and peace of mind. Notice in this passage, how the Lord does not want to further burden the righteous parents. The angel commanded them only to flee to Egypt and to "stay there until I bring you word." It means continue there, do not remove elsewhere, and do not return until I speak with you or order and command you otherwise. In other words, how much you need to know for further revelation will come in due time.

Another point that was not revealed was His purpose: though He was born to die for the sins of His people, His time had not yet come. He was to grow up to years of maturity and to fulfill the ultimate purpose of His incarnation, to do many miracles and at last to lay down His life, voluntarily, for all of mankind.

Again, the lesson we learn is to not plan far ahead, for God is merciful and may conceal His plan from us. The way will unfold step by step so leave tomorrow's burden with Christ. He is the only great burden bearer—the Lamb of God who bears the sin of the world.

St. Joseph: Head of the Holy Family

Family troubles occur nowadays when we do not emulate a saintly model such as St. Joseph's exemplary leadership of the Holy Family. His role as the pillar of his family and chaste guardian of the Virgin had been preplanned by the divine providence. No other book can enlighten us of the role of gigantic men like St. Joseph except the Bible, which tells us, "You search the Scriptures; for in them you think you have eternal life; and these are they which testify of Me" (John 5:39).

The absence of the traditional role of the husband as the head of the household has become a sad reality. Various toxic ideologies so rampant today have brought disorder into the home. A fatherless generation suffers from the lack of male headship, which creates a vacuum and either the mother has to fill or no one could possibly fill. When a father or husband fails his responsibilities, it affects the well-being of the whole family. In my book about the family, *The Exemplarily Upbringing of the Child*, I wrote that I have not found a better example of husband and father than the saintly model of St. Joseph. The book was all about this saint, his character, his simplicity, and his righteous life. If you ask, what books have been written by St. Joseph? The answer is none. What countries did he travel to as a missionary? The answer is also none. He was just a humble man worked as a carpenter. He probably spent most of his time in a carpentry workshop in Palestine, while other saints traveled the world serving, teaching, and preaching and died as missionaries.

According to the information we have, Joseph never preached and never wrote a single word, and we are not aware of any special talents in healing people. He did not perform miracles and was not a martyr. His life was simple and hidden, according to what has been revealed to us. But St. Joseph was definitely more than just a carpenter; he was a saint with great faith, and he was chosen by divine providence for the greatest task in history, to protect and take good care of the Son of God. He will continue be the best teacher, the finest character, the greatest model for all of us to emulate and raise our own families in these difficult times and at all times.

The following are the virtues of St. Joseph that we can start cultivating and emulating. To make it easier to remember, I will list them according to the spelling of his name: J, justice; O, obedience; S, silence; E, enabler; P, patience; H, humility. May we have the will, determination, and prayers of St. Joseph to lead us to love our families and like him learn to cultivate these great virtues and raise our own holy families. Amen.

Chapter Two

THE COMPASSIONATE LORD SAYS, "DO NOT WEEP"

"Young Man, I say to you arise."
—Luke 7:13–14

As Jesus approached the gate of the city called Nain, a man who had died "was being carried out, the only son of his mother; and she was a widow" (Luke 7:12). The death of a widow's only son meant that her only source of livelihood was gone. His death meant her abject poverty and premature death. In the Old Testament, the story of Naomi in Ruth tells of what was associated with the death of sons in biblical times. After losing both her husband and her two sons, Naomi laments, "Do not call me Naomi [that is, pleasant], call me Mara [that is, bitter]" (Ruth 1:20). Losing her only son meant he was gone—dead, silent forever—and she was alone until the moment when Jesus reached out to comfort her.

The Bible tells us when Jesus saw the widow, He had compassion for her and said to her, "Do not weep." How many times have we comforted loved ones with those very words? These words mean well and may seem consoling, but they neither remove the cause of the hurt nor the reason for the weeping. However, Jesus did more than offer compassionate words; He resurrected the widow's son from death. "And he who was dead sat up and began to speak... Then fear came upon all, and they glorified God." We can be sure that things were never the same, and the crowd was caught up in wonder, saying, "A great prophet has risen up among us" and "God has visited His people" (Luke 7: 15–16).

We all know that physical death brings sorrow, because when we lose someone we love, it makes us sad. Even Jesus felt the sorrow of losing a loved one. When He saw Martha, Mary, and their companions mourning after Lazarus died, "Jesus wept" (John 11:32–35). That is why death is referred to as an enemy (1 Cor. 15:25–26). Gratefully, Jesus, by His death, freed us from the fear of death and the bondage that it brings (Heb. 2:14–15).

Compassionate Attitude

Compassion, as we have witnessed in Jesus's tender loving care, is an emotional response and attitude toward others that is deeply empathetic. People generally respond to others in four ways: with apathy, antipathy, sympathy, or empathy. Sympathy is limited to the ability to share someone's feelings of sorrow in the face of sad incidents or misfortune. Empathy means to connect to human suffering with care and understand other people's feelings as if we were having them ourselves, then acting in ways that bring comfort to those around us. Let us opt to cultivate an empathetic attitude at all times.

Behind Every Saint, a Saintly Woman

In October 2018, Pope Tawadros II spoke boldly about this very subject while in the United States. He pointed to the importance of compassionate relationships with our neighbors, in our families, and in our communities. It is the state of being affectionate, warmhearted, and loving to those who cross our path. He pointed out how St. Monica, through her patience, perseverance, grace, and compassion, converted her pagan and abusive husband to Christianity before his death. After that, she lived a prayerful life until she converted her son Augustine to Christianity. Not only he had been converted to Christianity but he also was ordained a bishop and eventually was canonized a saint.

Referring to the same concept of compassion as a family virtue, Pope Francis came to Philadelphia in September 2015 for the World

Meeting of Families. Extolling the precious qualities of marital love, devotion, and loyalty, his focus was on being compassionate. Families who led successful lives enriched by devotion, shared their testimonials with millions on that evening, and they were uplifting, even magical. The pope actually joked that some would say, "Since you were never married, you could not know about marriage." The crowd smiled and laughed when he said that he "understood marital anger and the throwing of dishes."

Cultivating Compassion in the Family

Compassion is distinguished from empathy and sympathy. It is the ability to cultivate and practice a gentle way of thinking and being, if possible, all the time. To be compassionate, we must possess an attitude of concern for those who suffer as well spontaneous readiness to help and benefit others. Difficult encounters with family members, peers, and friends present opportunities for us to put ourselves in another's shoes—to practice empathy. That means to be compassionate in giving without the need to gain anything in return when we are with people or animals that are suffering and when we experience the internal reward of feeling appreciated.

Understand and Cope with Anger

One of the greatest hindrances to compassion is anger, because it can overwhelm our minds and spirit. At times, we may get angry, and we have to learn to manage our anger by addressing its causes in an appropriate manner. Holding on to anger leads to unreliable and destructive outcomes. Many things can trigger anger when facing family problems, financial issues, and other forms of stress. One must learn to "self-regulate" by thinking before speaking; once in state of calm, one may express his or her reasons for anger in a proper manner. It is also important not to hold a grudge. Always practice to releasing tension by daily exercise and using humor whenever you can.

Antidotes to anger come through compassion and self-regulation, meaning the ability to stop or delay an action rather than behave impulsively. We need to understand that regulating our anger is not a sign of weakness. Instead, a compassionate attitude is an internal strength. Cultivating a spirit of volunteering to serve others whenever we can help to develop our compassionate muscles.

Chapter Three

CULTIVATING AN ATTITUDE OF GRATITUDE

Although they knew God, they did not glorify
Him as God, nor were thankful.
—Romans 1:21

I read that a small boy who had learned the virtue of gratitude visited his friend's home for dinner. When the younger sat down at the table, he bowed his head and waited for someone to give thanks for the meal. The others at the table, however, began passing the food. The boy looked up and said, "You guys are just like my dog. You start right in!"[41]

Giving thanks takes the place of blessing as used by other evangelists. However, the word is used with intentional significance, most likely with marked reference to the paschal meal, at which thanksgiving plays so important part. There is a striking resemblance indeed between the description of John 6:11 and what followed later in the chapter (John 6:23) of the accounts of the Last Supper, especially that given in (1 Cor. 11:23–26).

Our focus today, though, is on cultivating an attitude of gratitude. Giving thanks is an expression of gratitude, which is a mark of developing spiritual maturity. Building this wonderful attitude takes effort, patience, and perseverance. It is something we learn to grow into. Therefore, it is our responsibility as parents to teach our children to be thankful and content. Teaching children to learn to be content takes place only through emulation, not by instruction. Telling them how to do it is an example of external learning soon to be forgotten. But if we do it and they witness our conduct day in and day out, they will follow in our footsteps via emulation or imitation.

One great benefit of learning to give thanks is the virtue of contentment. Contentment is an inexhaustible treasure. Being content means you're happy regardless of the state you are in, whether you are healthy or otherwise, accepted or rejected, loved or hated. Being content doesn't stop you, though, from trying to achieve, excel, and improve your situation.

The starting point for building such a gracious attitude is at mealtime as Jesus did, giving thanks. Every time we sit to eat alone or with our family, we bow our heads and give thanks, then watch how the blessings of the Lord abound as He did in feeding the five thousand from five loaves and a couple small fish to the amazement of the crowed. When they had seen what Jesus did, they said, "This is truly the Prophet who is to come into the world" (John 6:14).

The apostle Paul told Timothy that all food should be received with thanksgiving and appreciation to God (1 Tim. 4:4–5). Food has been given to us for nourishment and enjoyment. Our expression of thanks acknowledges that what we eat is a gift from God. In Paul's letter to the growing Christian in Ephesus, his challenge to follow Christ included "giving thanks always for all things to God the Father in the name of our Lord Jesus Christ" (Eph. 5:20). Apostle Paul also wrote to his friends in Rome, singling out the sin of ingratitude among the pagans. He said, "Although they knew God, they did not glorify Him as God, nor were thankful" (Rom. 1:21).

Today, let's practice thankfulness to God instead of complaining about what we don't have, instead of fuming about the unfairness of life, and instead of asking for more for ourselves.

Chapter Four

CULTURE OF MORAL RELATIVISM

Therefore take heed that the light which is in you is not darkness.
—Luke 11:35

The Light of the Son of Man

Luke's passage above is a warning that calls for self-scrutiny. It compels us to examine our beliefs and observe our conduct in the light of the Gospel. The "lamp of the body" is the eye that receives the light. "Therefore take heed that the light which is in you be not darkness" (Luke 11:34–35).

We live in a culture of "moral relativism" that views moral judgments as true or false only to some particular standpoint. Moral relativism in its most radical form is the doctrine that truth depends not on the way things are but solely on what someone believes or someone's culture believes. Regretfully, the New Age movement that started in the 1970s has apparently been adopted by a whole generation of college students. They call it "relativism" referring to new way of thinking in which they claim there is no objective, external standard for right and wrong that is valid for everyone. The church and Christian believers consider relativism as denial of absolute truth, which leads to the denial of sin and God.

This is a far cry from the story we read of an affectionate and honest woman who discovered the truth in Jesus. Upon hearing His excellent discourses, the woman raised her voice and said to the Lord, "Blessed is the womb that bore you, and the breasts that nursed you"

(Luke 11:27). The woman had discovered the truth in the Lord. The truth here is not something, it is somebody. That somebody is the one who says, "I am the way, the truth, and the life" (John 14:6). He is our standard of measure by which we can judge ourselves and others. He is the absolute truth that all what He says is true at all times and in all places. His truth is always true no matter what the circumstances. It is a fact that cannot be changed, altered, or debated. His absolute truths existed and continue to exist in all cultures and everywhere on earth or in heaven.

Jesus Is the One and Only Truth

The woman's high esteem for Christ and the way she reflected honor upon the Virgin Mary, his mother, was well said. "But He said, 'More than that, [or more than the honor that bestowed on His mother] blessed are those who hear the word of God and keep it'" (Luke 11:28). Then He said, "This is an evil generation. It seeks a sign, and no sign will be given to it... The queen of the south will rise up in the judgment with the men of this generation and condemn them" (Luke 11:29, 31). We may be amazed by that evil generation, but I dare say that the queen of Sheba and the men of Nineveh would have risen up in judgment against this generation of our time and the ones that follow and would have condemned them as well.

For behold the Lord Jesus who is greater than Jonah and far wiser than Solomon is here. But the world around us is blinded and darkened in mind, heart, and soul. They have eyes but don't see and ears but don't hear. They believe in and practice a culture of death, paganism, and egotism and are driven by a desire for power and prestige. If the Lord Jesus declared that the generation of Pharisees and scribes was an evil generation, I wonder what He would say of this generation that believes in "moral relativism." This ideology holds that nobody is objectively right or wrong, and because nobody is right or wrong, we ought to tolerate the behavior of others even when we disagree with the morality of it.

The Faithful Mission

What is our role then? We all have to have a mission and take it seriously. Our mission is what the Lord has instructed for us—to be the salt of the earth and the light of the world and to let our light shine before men so that they may see our good works and glorify our Father who is in heaven. In other words, we don't just live out our faith inside the walls of our churches and of our homes. We're not to be of the world, but we're to be *in* the world. We're citizens of an earthly kingdom as well as a heavenly one. Citizens participate in their culture, everything from what children are taught in school to what appears on TV screens to what is communicated through social media.

Let's make sure, then, that the eye of the soul sees clear, sees things as they are, and judges impartially concerning them. As a result, the whole body, that is, the whole soul, is full of light. It receives and entertains the Gospel, which will bring into the soul both knowledge and joy. St. Dorotheus of Gaza explains it further:

> When God made human beings, he put in them a kind of divine faculty, more alive and splendid than a spark, to illuminate the spirit and show it the difference between good and evil. It is the conscience with that law which is part of its nature. The patriarchs and all the saints were able to please God by obeying the law of conscience. But people tramped on it and muddied it with their sinfulness. As a consequence we needed a written law, we needed the prophets, we needed the actual coming of our Lord Jesus to rediscover, to re-awaken, to rekindle in us the spark which had been smothered.[42]

Chapter Five

EXCLUSIVE BIBLICAL DISCIPLINE

The Christian does not think God will love us because we are good, but that God will make us good because He loves us.
—C. S. Lewis

Christian families who want to raise children in fear of the Lord are always looking for loving ways to discipline their children in a misguided world. Could we protect them while they are frequently surrounded by unethical friends or find themselves immersed in an immoral, corrupt culture? The tsunami of the digital age with its powerful attractions exposes them to evil images, negative ideologies, and inappropriate language to say the least. They are subject to all these contaminations even while in the privacy of their homes. Obstacles families face include violence and other safety concerns, emotional or behavioral dysfunction, bullying online and in schools, drugs and addiction, and toxic stress.

Today's soaring rates of crime, school dropouts, and depression and anxiety suggest that the current crop of child-education and child-rearing experts have got it wrong. These are crucial concerns and questions that demand answers and our immediate attention. Yet when rearing children, there are no better answers than biblical guidance and reliable Christian themes. Telling them, "If you cannot do it, we will teach you; if you don't want to, we'll force you" or "You must listen to me because I say so!" will only result in distasteful back talk like, "It's a free country!" with a know-it-all sneer. Such conflicts unfortunately have become familiar in many families today.

So then, how can biblical discipline be applied? We find in the scripture a certain righteous path that is different from what the secular world offers us, although the biblical guidance is affirmed by what behavioral health scientists are saying about a child's spiritual development. They actually have emphasized through scientific research the importance of spirituality in nourishing our children's well-being. But most importantly, parents can learn how to make it happen through biblical discipline.

Dr. Lisa Miller, in her book *The Spiritual Child: The New Science of Parenting for Health and Lifelong Thriving*, writes,

> Science also shows that while we are born with inherent spirituality, this faculty can be sustained and cultivated by parents or dulled by neglect. In the past two decades our lab and those of colleagues around the country have conducted pioneering scientific research to define the pathway of spiritual development, how it can be supported by parents, and related benefits to children's wellness and thriving into adulthood.[43]

As we reflect on what science says about the spiritual child, it behooves us to search the inspired scripture:

In Hebrews 12:1–11, our merciful God shows us how He treats and disciplines His children. Parents who study the Bible daily will learn from God's guidance. As they follow His counseling, they too will learn to guide and discipline their children. Speaking of perseverance, St. Paul says, "You have not yet resisted to bloodshed, striving against sin (Heb. 12:4). He reminds the Hebrews that God calls them "sons" and encourages them as He says, "My son, do not despise the chastening of the Lord, nor be discouraged when you are rebuked by Him; For whom the Lord loves he chastens, And scourges every son whom He receives" (Heb. 12:5–6). The apostle Paul acknowledges that they are going through a hard time (as parents and children go through today) and asks them to endure God's discipline.

It is only because God delights in His children that He discipline them. Then St. Paul gets to his main lesson, which is to endure hardships as discipline because God deals with you as with sons, for what son is not disciplined by his father? If you are not disciplined, then you are illegitimate children and not true sons. Moreover, we have all had human fathers who corrected us, and we respected them, for their guidance was out of love and care. Of course, as Paul says in his epistle to the Hebrews, no discipline seems pleasant at the time but rather is painful. Later on, however, it produces a harvest of righteousness and peace for those who received it" (Heb. 12:11).

So we must compassionately discipline our children and do it selflessly with the right attitude, being in control of our emotions. Thus, we set up boundaries for behavior and consequences that focus on the child's best outcome. As such, we are expressing love exactly as God sometimes expresses His love. The child may complain and resist, he or she may make things quite uncomfortable for both the parent and the child in the moment, but in the long run, it is the most compassionate thing a parent can do to set the child up for success in life and joy in His kingdom.

In conclusion, it behooves us to reflect on our compassionate Lord Jesus, who says the following as quoted in *The Imitation of Christ.*

THE VOICE OF CHRIST

My child, I came down from heaven for your salvation and took upon Myself your miseries, not out of necessity but out of love, that you might learn to be patient and bear the suffering of this life without repining. From the moment of My birth to My death on the cross, suffering did not leave Me. I suffered great want of temporal goods. Often I heard many complaints against Me. Disgrace and reviling I bore with patience. For My blessings I received ingratitude, for My Miracles blasphemies, and for My teaching scorn.[44]

Chapter Six

EXEMPLARY FAMILY CARE
FOR THE ELDERLY

*You shall rise before the gray headed and honor the presence
of an old man, and fear your God: I am the Lord.*

—Leviticus 19:32

In today's society, we are all so busy earning a living, busy with ourselves and our needs, and even busy in church activities, yet we have
no time for those who most need our love, care, and attention. How
sad it is that there are people who live in our midst who are lonely
and in need of our love and tender care as they miss even a smile and
a word of comfort. Not being able to provide "at home" family care
has an impact, because then the elderly are forced to live in nursing
homes and other facilities. Regardless of the type of care available
there, any visitor to these places will see the sheer misery written all
over residents' faces. The moment they step into one of these places,
they lose their identity.

I read the story of an American reporter in China who once
asked a poor farmer, "What makes you endure the miserable life and
austerity of your condition here rather than joining your son who is
doing well in America?"

The Chinese farmer bowed to him and said, "Sir, I once was
there to visit my son and was stunned how rich the Americans are,
but I found them to be very poor indeed!"

The reporter, shocked at his answer, asked, "How so?"

The farmer replied with a sad expression on his face, "Your elderly go to nursing homes when they became frail and need the love and care of their own family members. Those who are not in nursing homes live by themselves secluded, lonely, and sad as they are unable to enjoy family life when they most need it!"

Against all odds, Coptic families still provide tender loving care to their elderly at home. Even members whose their circumstances limit their ability to provide care at home still visit their elderly daily to spend time with them, feeding them and keeping their company as well providing personal supplies that are not available at the facility. Most importantly, they keep their spiritual life intact. Coptic priests are amazingly caring, and with love they nourish the spiritual lives of our elderly family members whether at home or in a nursing facility, helping them partake in the Holy Communion. Some of these caring families ought to be inducted into Coptic Community Hall of Fame. Here, we are honored to give just a couple examples, because many of us have witnessed and been touched by their exemplarily manner in dealing with the frail older members of their family.

The first is the family of the Very Rev. Fr. Roufail Youssef and his wife, Tasoni Suzan, in caring for her father, the (late) Very Rev. Fr. Bassellious Sedrak. Fr. Bassellious is a "champion" priest who suffered persecution, intimidation, and imprisonment in Egypt during the reign of President Anwar Sadat in the 1980s. The crackdown also affected other priests, bishops, Christian politicians, and distinguished laity. In November 1988, His Holiness Pope Shenouda III appointed Fr. Bassellious as a priest for St. Mary and St. Abraam Coptic Orthodox Church in Saint Louis, Missouri. He also was given the temporary responsibility to serve at St. Mark and St. Bishoy in Chicago. Soon after his arrival in Saint Louis, the church building construction project took off. It was completed in 1994 and later consecrated by the late Pope Shenouda III.

Fr. Bassellious was a noble and loving priest who, after many fruitful years dedicated to shepherding his congregation, lost his wife and lived alone. He suddenly fell while by himself and suffered partial paralysis. After his discharge from the hospital, he was transferred to live with his daughter Tasoni Suzan in Pennsylvania. She and her husband, Fr. Roufail, and their family took upon themselves the responsibility to care for her father at their home. Fr. Bassellious was disabled and frail, thus requiring 24/7 care. Yet the family refused to place him in a nursing home. He lived with them for more than seven years.

Their home became an extension of himself. It was a refuge and represented family life, familial continuity, and generational relationships nurtured over a lifetime that gave Fr. Bassellious substance and meaning. His life as a priest never stopped even during his disability. He was brought weekly to participate in the Holy Liturgy as well other church worship activities and lived in communion with Jesus until the day he departed earthly life.

The second example is the Farid Mansour family. Mr. Mansour was a distinguished engineer who, through his technical and professional accomplishments, occupied prestigious positions in his field in several states. He also was a deacon and zealous servant who served his church well and represented the congregation on the church's board of deacons as a vice president and secretary for many years. Mr. Mansour was the overseer of church maintenance and, with his counterpart Mr. Nazih Makary, acted as consultant to the priests in purchasing land, finalizing required construction drawings, and thus mastering the planning phase and designs for the new church building in Plymouth Meeting, Pennsylvania.

Mr. Mansour loved the youth in the church and taught Coptic Church history in Sunday school servants' meetings. He also loved people in general, especially his Coptic community, and catered to their needs and supported them in their struggles for years. His wife, who also was an engineer by profession, was his right hand in his service while raising two wonderful children, now accomplished and professional adults, thus shaping a lovely and righteous family.

Mrs. Mansour, a dedicated servant who spends most of her professional life serving the church, has been leading the agape celebration at St. George Church after the Holy Liturgy on Sundays. *Agape*, a Greek word, means "unconditional love," and *samiha*, meaning "cheerful" in Arabic, is an unconditionally loving person, wife, and mother! Her love engulfs the entire Coptic community. She has been a vital part of several church activities, including fundraising, weddings, conferences, annual youth spiritual contests and festivals, and even memorial services. The St. George Church congregation and both Fr. Roufail and Fr. Mina Shaheid presented Mrs. Mansour with several noteworthy awards in recognition of her unceasing and generous service through the years.

Regretfully, Mr. Mansour developed physical limiting conditions later in his life. Though he had always been energetic and physically able, he started to suffer from a gradual decline in health. The onset of chronic pain and the medication to deal with it led to reduced mobility and greater dependency. Mr. Mansour was able, though, to buffer the deleterious effects of his progressively limited ability to function. Through strong family support, networking connections, adaptive equipment, and medical health care provided at his residence, he was able to receive treatment and stay at home.

The crux of the matter is that Mrs. Mansour championed these efforts and provided 24/7 care for her husband rather than placing him in a nursing home or even a rehab facility. For almost two years, Mrs. Mansour single-handedly coordinated his treatment in the comfort of their home while surrounded by family and visiting friends and loved ones. During the time of this ordeal, Mr. Mansour never complained or lost his spiritual vitality. He discussed his faith and hope in the Lord with his visitors, attending physicians, nurses, and other healthcare workers assigned to his care. Not only did he proclaim his faith with friends and strangers alike, he also managed to write about his pain and suffering and published a book titled *Blessings of Pains*. The Coptic community celebrated his departure on July 18, 2020. May his soul rest in peace.

The Main Message

The Lord Jesus will not walk once again in the flesh to find the elderly, the frail, and the sick; He assigned this role to you and me, his children…sons and daughters who know Him and not just about Him, who love Him not in words but in action and deed, and who gladly serve Him.

A Noble Event Worth Noting

Jefferson Medical Care Program in Nursing Homes

A Novel Approach and Application

Through the leadership of Thomas Jefferson Medical College at Thomas Jefferson University and the Pennsylvania Department of Aging, an extensive mental health and medical program was launched. The program's mission was to alleviate the pain, mental anguish, and suffering of frail elderly residents in nursing home facilities. As a faculty member at the Department of Psychiatry of Human Behavior, I joined a team of medical experts to make a change in the lives of the elderly in nursing homes and life-care facilities in Philadelphia area and beyond. The program over the years was successful and drew extensive national media attention.

Philadelphia Inquirer reporter Darrell Sifford wrote an extensive article about it in the early 1970s. He specialized in writing about family relationships and fear of aging. Sifford witnessed the unique care provided by the Thomas Jefferson Medical College program for the elderly. In the two-page article, he spoke about the grim future of residents secluded in the facility. As one of these residents said to him, "I know when I get out of this place I'll be in my coffin!"

Sifford wrote that the Jefferson medical team thought it should not have to be this way. The program included "freeing the residents" from the grip of loneliness and depression while secluded from their families and loved ones for the "rest of their lives." Besides providing medical and mental healthcare, the team arranged for day trips for the nursing home residents. Charter buses transported them safely and reliably to many new places or old favorites the residents requested. These trips were sponsored by local businesses as an early example of corporate social responsibility (CSR). Beside its mission of basic care, the Jefferson program offered the frail nursing home residents a chance to break away from their daily routine.

By opening their minds to life outside their facilities, it engaged and restored their sense of freedom from the grip of institutional isolation. The purpose of these trips was to complement their medical treatment by improving their mental and emotional health. After each trip, they returned at the end of the day feeling rejuvenated and more relaxed. But the most important aspect of these trips was to reconnect with family members they had not seen for a long time. Many members of their families welcomed the idea and found these trips an opportunity to meet their institutionalized elders outside their care facilities.

The nursing home facilities were also very supportive, preparing lunches for the residents and assigning staff support to care for them during the trip. Recreation staff planned activities to have them sing along, share jokes, and have fun. All these trips contributed to the betterment of their health, expanded their social circle, and encouraged their engagement. It also was documented that the program improved their quality of life, curbed cognitive decline, and alleviated depression. Connecting once again with their family members and the outside world made them feel anchored in the here and now. They felt they belonged and were appreciated by their family and societal support, which went a long way toward a more positive and healthier life in their sunset years.

Chapter Seven

IMITATING CHRIST IN DISCIPLING

He who says he abides in Him ought himself
also to walk just as He walked.

—1 John 2:6

Modeling Christ's Nobility

As believers, we are to follow the example of Christ. To imitate Him is to copy His action as closely as possible. It is to model our lives after the characteristics of the one we love and look up to. As children of God through faith in Christ, we are to imitate Him. We are to learn to observe His way of speaking, caring, and relating to people. From Him, we learn how to respond to the many circumstances of life. Spending time with Him in prayer and learning about Him in the Bible, we will want to imitate His nobility as a way of life.

When we speak about relationships, it should be based on the know-how to connect, communicate, and interact with other human beings. With the rules for relating to one another by imitating Christ, we're being judged by a new yardstick—not how intelligent we are, or how much education or skills we may have, but how well we handle ourselves and each other as Jesus taught us. Most of our learning style comes first from modeling after parents and/or significant others. Another source of learning is "environmental learning" and the impact of behavior modification during the developmental stages of our lives.

150

Nobility in Communication

We, as Christians, prefer to use a biblical style of communication as our frame of reference in certain situations rather than rely on other behavioral science resources that may not be accessible or could easily be forgotten. Role modeling was an important part of Jesus's ministry, and as Christians, our job is to be that role model. When we relate to those who cross our path in life, we ought to learn how to replicate the communication style of the Lord when He spoke with the Samaritan woman (John 4:4–26).

Methodology Steps of Communication

The following are the steps to follow to imitate this noble style of communication.

First, setting the stage. Anytime we communicate, we need to (1) stop to cool down if we are upset; (2) set a place, time, and person with whom we want to address an issue; (3) learn the art of initiation. Now let us apply this to the story of the Samaritan woman as illustrated in John 4:1–26.

Application process. You will notice that Jesus, being tired from His journey, *stopped to rest* and sat by Jacob's well (*place*). We, too, when tired must stop and cool down before addressing any issue of concern with someone, especially with our spouse after a long day of work or during overwhelming events that may occupy our mind. You can't just barge in to discuss an issue that the other person may not have the slightest idea about or at least not be ready to discuss.

Jesus also chose the sixth hour (*time*) when no one was at the well; even His disciples had gone away. He wanted to address her one-on-one and not embarrass her. He also knew who would come to the well and what kind of a person she was and the life she led at that time. Once she came to draw water, he said to her, "Give Me a drink" (*Initiation*). Engaging others in dialogue requires charitable attitude, sincerity, and a good reason for such initiation.

Second, respond and reconcile. Whenever discussing any issue, we need to make sure to (1) not react but instead acknowledge the other person's concern, (2) listen to understand, and (3) prop, praise, and validate.

Application process. We find Jesus *responding and reconciling* as the Samaritan woman took a harsh "how dare you!" attitude, or in her own words, "How is it that you being a Jew, ask a drink from me a Samaritan woman?" Jesus, who knew why she asked the question, *listened and understood* but moved on to reconcile with her. It was not the time to discuss race or ethnicity; it was a time to speak about God's gift of the living water.

Empathetic listing is an important part of any communication. However, it will not be effective unless there is a sincere desire to understand. We as followers and servants ought to imitate Jesus's style of responsiveness and reconciliation. Our objective is quite clear to listen and understand and "to do His will...and to finish His work." All is done within a frame of gentle words, charitable attitude, and empathy.

The art of communication, however, will never be complete without practicing and applying the *propping* technique. Even if we are quite knowledgeable or familiar with the individual's circumstances, we ought to give him or her the time to verbalize and express their concern and let the person "unload" at their level of comfort. That is what Jesus did when He said to the Samaritan woman, "Go, call your husband, and come here." When the woman said, "I have no husband." Jesus *praised* her honesty, saying, "You have well said." He actually looked for some positive attributes that would enhance her self-image, which was clothed with a sense of shame and hurt. She found out that He knew she had five husbands and "the one whom you now have is not your husband." The Lord then *validated* her truthfulness "in that you spoke truly."

Third, staying on the subject, means to (1) resolve one issue at a time, (2) refrain from bringing in past incidents, and (3) keep it simple.

Application process. In any discussion, let us strive to *resolve the one issue* at hand that would obviously require *staying on the subject* and not deviating from it. A sincere intention to find an agreeable solution eliminates conflict, misunderstanding, and ill feelings. Several times the Samaritan woman opted to change the subject, moving from one issue to another, but Jesus, though supportive, remained steadfast. In addition to staying on the subject, one has to make sure to *refrain from bringing up past negative issues* or revisiting painful experiences with the one who caused it, unless both parties agree to revisit such issues for healing purposes. The key ingredient is to *keep it simple*, one issue at a time.

Fourth, finding solution. When both parties are ready to discuss or revisit unresolved matter, it is important to (1) agree on the problem, (2) brainstorm solutions, and (3) commit and follow up.

In our clinical work, we always ask the client, "What do you think the problem is?" and write down the problem as stated in his or her own words. It is crucial to know and *agree on the problem* we are facing or want to resolve. People often hide their feelings behind a wall of words. They use a kind of double-talk in which words and feelings do not agree.

In daily clinical practice, we find many people are afraid that honesty in speech will cost them friendship, love, or respect. So they either keep their lips zipped or say something other than what they mean. Therefore, when conflict and tension surface, people tend to hide how they really feel, and that is why recognizing the problem should be crystal clear.

Once the parties involved agree on the problem, the next step is to *brainstorm solutions*. The behavioral health field, we have also noticed that people may express their opinion a little too emphatically in their zeal to solve a problem. In their enthusiasm to make a point, they may be inclined to speak loudly and with great animation. As a result, people may appear angry when actually they are not.

Application process. In the story of the Samaritan woman, at first it seems the problem is a rift between the Samaritans and the Jews and their hatred to each other. Later, the conflict between both tribes over where each worships, whether on the mountain or in Jerusalem, is brought up. Jesus, who knows the problem and is quite aware of the ill feelings it causes between Jews and Samaritans, *resolved* each of the issues separately. He at first draws her attention by asking for a drink. Then He introduces her to the living water and says "whoever drinks of the water that I shall give him will never thirst" (John 4:14).

As far as which place of worship it ought to be, the Lord assures her: "Woman, believe Me, the hour is coming when you will neither on this mountain, nor in Jerusalem, worship the Father." Not only does the Lord resolve each issue separately, He also guides her to bring out differences and concerns between Jews and Samaritans, then gives her the precise solutions. He says to her, "You worship what you do not know; we know what we worship, for the salvation of the Jews" (John 4:21). The Lord would not stop there but instead *commit and follows up:* "But the hour is coming and now is when the true worshipers will worship the Father in Spirit and truth; for the Father is seeking such to worship Him… Those who worship Him must worship in spirit and truth" (John 4:23–24).

We are Christians who are honored to serve in the Lord's vineyard. Whether we're addressing a problem or trying to find a solution, we ought to remain sensitive toward all, especially peers and those we serve, and strive to be Christian models. We ought to be sensitive to the needs, hurts, and disappointments of others and ensure that no unkind words come from our lips and no harsh tone is heard in our voice. Sometimes within a relationship, though we aim to solve an issue, we need to realize that the window of time may not be enough or resistance may remain an obstacle.

Other factors that may impede straight talk are shyness, lack of confidence, fear of displaying ignorance, trying to avoid criticism, and not wanting to hurt someone's feelings. Here we commit ourselves to revisit the issue at a mutually agreed upon time and place, then follow up. When we do, "Let your speech always be with grace, seasoned with salt, that you may know how you ought to answer each one" (Col. 4:6).

In Conclusion

Earlier in this book, I shared the leader-servant mission and vision as an overarching aspiration of what we hope to achieve. Our mission should be to serve, educate, affirm, and inspire new generations. With God's grace, strive to motivate those we serve and— if possible—engage all those who cross our path to serve the Lord.

Not only contribute zealously to serving Him but also extending His kingdom on earth. In serving and proclaiming the word, there is one specific rule to endure, keeping in mind that people will listen carefully if they see us living faithfully.

So what is this one rule to be cognizant of? The fact that there is only one teacher. To the degree we become one with Jesus the only teacher, we will be able to teach. To the degree we become one with the truth, we will be able to impart the truth. The truth has two dimensions: objective reality and subjective reality. Objective reality is the word, the Bible, also known as ontological truth based upon being or existence. Subjective reality is based on what's on one's mind and is perceived and conditioned by one's own personal views and desires.

In imitating Christ, we see that in His encounter with the Samaritan woman, the Lord shows us a beautiful example of God's love and total acceptance. Jesus went out of His way to find and offer this woman by the well a place in His heart and His kingdom. A woman who appears an outcast in her own town becomes the first of His disciples. Through His noble style of kindness, gentleness, and empathetic communication style, He draws her to recognize Him first as a prophet. Then finally she says to Him, "'I know that Messiah is coming' (who is called Christ). 'When He comes, He will tell us all things'" (John 4:25).

Jesus said to her, "I who speak to you am He." The Samaritan woman went her way into the city and said to the men, "Come, see." Not only did she become His first disciple after He reached out to her but also, she reached back. She proclaimed the good news then, and through this beautiful story in the Gospel of John, we wonder how many millions she has witnessed to over the centuries!

Chapter Eight

KEYS TO SUCCESSFUL RELATIONSHIPS

Try not to become a person of success, but to become a person of value.
—Albert Einstein

The Problem-Solving Key

Looking carefully at people's lives through research and clinical practice and examining their pains and agony, I realized that many so-called problem-solving techniques are only temporary solutions. They are most of the time quick fixes to deep-seated problems. Sometimes these fixes and/or social Band-Aids appear to solve them superficially, but they leave the underlying chronic problem unresolved to fester and resurface time and time again.

The Personality Traits Key

Scientists in the late twentieth century and some behaviorists until recently believed that success was more a function of personality, charismatic image, attitudes and behaviors, skills and techniques that enhance the process of human interaction and human attraction. Some even spoke of what is known as positive mental attitude (PMA) and "your attitude determines your altitude." Indeed PMA, personal growth, and good communication skills are important personality traits, but they are secondary, not primary, traits for success-ful living.

The Neighbor's Welfare Key

This is a version of the golden rule, "Do unto others as you would have them do unto you." We all heard the commandment "love your neighbor as yourself," and no doubt we all want to honor God by being hospitable, kind, and loving with no strings attached. Jesus tells in the parable of the Good Samaritan (Luke 10:25–37) to illustrate this commandment. However, this is a far cry from the idiomatic cultural expression, "What's in it for me?"

The "Bag of Cookies" Story

Let me share a story titled "The Cookie Thief!" by Valerie Cox that has been circulated on YouTube and the internet. A young exec-utive waiting to board her flight in the airport decided to buy a bag of cookies, then sit and read her favorite novel until departure time. She placed her bag of cookies on a small corner table that separated her from another person who sat beside her. She started reading her book, and once in a while she would grab a cookie from her bag, but to her surprise, she noticed the other person doing the same. Every time she took a cookie, he did the same. She became irritated, frustrated, and increasingly angry as this stranger dared to eat her cookies.

She thought repeatedly to stop him or even insult him for his inappropriate behavior and flawed character but restrained herself. She entertained the idea that it was better to ignore him and not engage in a fruitless conversation. But what made her most mad was when there was only one cookie left in the bag, he had the audacity to take it, then share it by breaking it in half and leaving the other half in the bag for her. That was too much to take; she got up fuming with anger and left her seat.

Later on, as she sat comfortably in her seat on the plane, she continued to be angry about the whole incident, blaming herself for failing to reprimand him then and there. She finally dismissed the whole matter and opened her handbag to get her book out to continue reading. Suddenly she was filled with shame—the bag of cookies she had bought in the airport was there, unopened. Realizing that *she* was the one who preyed on the bag of cookies and not the other way around, she belittled herself and felt small and ashamed.

She then sprang up and walked down the aisle, hoping to see his face among the passengers so she could offer him her sincere apology and pay her respect to this kind, tender, caring and undemanding gentleman who gladly shared his cookies without uttering a word or expecting a thank-you from the stranger who ate his cookies and walked away. Crushed and disappointed, she sat back in her seat with tears running down her cheeks to write her short story.

The moral of this story is that the way we see the problem is often the problem. The question now becomes, how can we see otherwise?

The Harmony Within Key

As I said earlier, personal growth, communication skills, and positive mental attitude are important personality traits, but they are secondary, not primary, traits for successful living. Successful living and our ability to avoid difficulties in life depends on individual harmony within. Indeed, difficulties in life are often caused by disharmony in the individual. Harmony within one's self means that the person chooses to accept all aspects of their personality. He lets all those characteristics work together to create inner tranquility and a grateful disposition.

Disharmony within usually stems from discord between mind, heart, and deeds. Our mental faculty, emotional needs, and satisfaction do not correspond with our morals, ethics, character, and behavior. The degree by which each of these faculties is openly and freely tuned with one another leads to a degree of perfect order and perfect harmony.

We pray every day, probably several times a day, the Our Father and always repeat, "Thy kingdom come. Thy will be done on earth as it is in heaven" His kingdom is supposed to be within us, and our role supported by His divine grace is to extend His kingdom on earth. We all believe there is no discord in His kingdom, only something unconquered in His children. The rule of His kingdom is perfect order, perfect harmony, perfect love, perfect honesty, perfect obedience—all power, all conquest, all success.

But so often, most if not all His children lack these powers, and we may think that the good Lord has not fulfilled His promises because these orderly and powerful attributes are not manifested in our lives. They are only manifested as a result to our obedience, honesty, humility, and love, and as the Lord Himself declares, these outward manifestations come not in answer to prayer but naturally as light results from a lighted candle. In *The Imitation of Christ* we read,

> A man is raised up from the earth by two wings—
> simplicity and purity. There must be simplicity in
> his intention and purity in his desires. Simplicity
> leads to God, purity embraces and enjoys him. If
> your heart be free from ill-ordered affection, no
> good deed will be difficult for you. If you aim at
> and seek after nothing but the pleasure of God
> and the welfare of your neighbor, you will enjoy
> freedom within.[45]

Chapter Nine

LEADERS' SHARED VISION ON EASTER

"I hope the day that all the Christians are one. This is my dream."
—Pope Tawadros II of Alexandria

Easter Celebrations in the Midst of Pandemic

On Easter Sunday of 2020, churches around the world celebrated Easter. The glorious day of Easter is a highly anticipated occasion during which Christians celebrate the resurrection of our savior, Jesus Christ. Because of His boundless love and His grace, our sins are forgiven. "Praise be to the Lord and Father of our Lord Jesus Christ! In his great mercy he has given us new birth into a living hope through the resurrection of Jesus Christ from the dead" (1 Peter 1:3). For the first time, however, Christians had to adjust to the circumstances due to the coronavirus pandemic and observed Easter via streaming online church services. Most families had to celebrate by making the maximum use of social media to exchange greetings and see each other.

Easter is celebrated by one Christian faith but on two different dates, or what may be called the inconsistency of two Easters. It has remained a thorny problem for the Christian Church. According to the World Council of Churches, "It has long been recognized that to celebrate this fundamental aspect of the Christian faith on different dates gives a divided witness and compromises the churches' credibility and effectiveness in bringing the Gospel to the world."

Despite challenges caused by the coronavirus pandemic that have taken a significant toll on the people of the world, one dares to say, "It is a great moment." It has been a unique opportunity for the Christian Church to speak in one voice. The message showed solidarity of purpose to eradicate the disease, alleviate people's fear, restore hope and peace. Christians and non-Christians in every country have been subjected to this mysterious virus that invades both healthy and not so healthy people. The result—crippling fear, high anxiety, lingering grief, and yes, the death of millions—is spreading viciously all over the world.

This invisible enemy shattered the economies of both wealthy and underdeveloped nations. People around the world are in the grip of suffering, and the emotional impact of lockdowns in response to the pandemic has been severe. They are unable to find work, earn a living, or support themselves and their families. In the face of this tragic pandemic, church leaders in every part of the world were united to alleviate the pain and suffering, praying and speaking in one voice to encourage people and rekindle their faith in our loving, caring God as merciful and omnipotent in His protection and might.

Historical Unity: Church Leaders with One Voice

Suddenly, thank God, the historical differences among churches came to a halt under these frightening circumstances. Conflicts pertaining to faith matters, tradition, practices, canon law, and church identity appeared to have been, if not completely eliminated, at least pushed aside. In an effort to save the lives of millions and restore unity and peace on earth, church leaders are now united with one message and strong voice encouraging people to earnestly pray for help and to support each other and find solutions to the devastation caused by this widespread virus. The plague of the coronavirus continues until this very day...

The late John Cardinal Krol in one of his speeches once said, "It is Christianity, vocal and active for time and place. It is the bridge and the bridge-builder between time and eternity... It gives meaning to the suffering of humanity, and through the alchemy of Divine Love it converts the crosses of human suffering into crucifixes of salvation."[46] As well, the following words of Pope Francis speak volumes about facing the danger of this "novel" coronavirus.

Pope Francis's 2020 Easter Vision

This is not a time for indifference, because the whole world is suffering and needs to be united in facing the pandemic.

—Pope Francis

In an editorial published on April 17, 2020, by the Spanish weekly religious magazine *Vida Nueva*, Pope Francis said Christians are called on to be joyful witnesses to Christ's victory over death during the coronavirus pandemic. The pope has presented "a plan for the rising up again" of humanity in the midst of a global crisis that has brought the world's peoples to their knees. He shared it in an exclusive meditation for *Vida Nueva*, in which he reflects on the coronavirus pandemic in the light of the resurrection of Jesus.

Excerpts of Pope Francis's "Rising Up" Plan

The pontiff shared his vision about the state of world suffering and expressed concern over the crisis caused by the pandemic. At the time of his writing, it had infected more than two million people and claimed the life of over 140,000 victims. The absence of an apparent solution and confusion resembles in many ways that of the disciples of Jesus after His death and burial in the tomb. Like them, "we live surrounded by an atmosphere of pain and uncertainty," and, Pope Francis said, like the women waiting at the tomb, we ask, "Who will roll away the stone?" He then, likens the stone that sealed the tomb of Jesus to the tombstones of the pandemic that "threatens to bury all hope" for the elderly living in total isolation, for families who lack food, and for those on the front lines of care who are "exhausted and overwhelmed."

Pope Francis says many are participating in the passion of Christ today, either personally or at the side of others, and he reminds everyone, "We are not alone. The Lord goes before us on our journey, and removes the stones that paralyze us." This is the hope that no one can take from us, he says. The pontiff considers it "a great moment" and a "propitious time" to be open to the Spirit, who can "inspire us with a new imagination of what is possible." He recalls that the Spirit does not allow itself "to be closed in or manipulated by fixed or outmoded methods or decadent structures" but rather moves us to "make new things."

Easter being a time to rise up with the risen Lord and with Him start new life, he says, "Easter calls us and invites us to remember this other discreet and respectful, generous and reconciling presence, so as to start that new life which is given to us." This presence "is the breath of the Spirit that opens horizons, sparks creativity, and renews brotherhood and makes us say, 'I'm present' in the face of the enormous and urgent task that awaits us."

At this moment in history, Pope Francis says, "We have recognized the importance of joining the entire human family in the search for a sustainable and integral development." We have also understood that "for better or worse all our actions affect others because everything is connected in our common home, and if the health authorities order that we remain confined in our home, it is the people who make this possible, aware of their co-responsibility in stopping the pandemic."

He insists that "an emergency like COVID-19 is overcome in the first place by the antibodies of solidarity." This lesson "breaks all the fatalism in which we have immersed ourselves and allows us to return to be the architects and protagonists of a common history," he says, and it enables us "to respond together to the many evils that are affecting so many of our brothers and sisters across the globe." To me, his talk of "the antibodies of solidarity" and responding in Christian care for "our brothers and sisters across the globe" is the key to his ecumenical message.

"We cannot allow ourselves to write the present and future history by turning our backs on the suffering of so many people," the pope says. Quoting the book of Genesis, he writes that God himself is asking us, "Where is your brother?" He expressed the hope that our response would be marked by "hope, faith and charity."[47]

Chapter Ten

POPE TAWADROS II 2020
EASTER HOMILY

This resurrection is proof that life is more powerful
than death, that love is greater than hate.

—Pope Tawadros II

Addressing fears and anxiety of the multitudes and the grieving souls of those who lost loved ones around the world, His Holiness Pope Tawadros II delivered a hopeful, consoling, and invigorating Easter homily of the Holy Resurrection the night before Sunday, April 19, 2020.

Excerpts of the Pope's Homily on Resurrection

Life Is More Powerful Than Death

Pope Tawadros II began by acknowledging the pandemic's impact on 2020's celebration for people around the world. "Yet this year we celebrate in a spiritual way with our families and in our homes, [not in churches] and this is wonderful," he said. Assuring his audience not to fear the physical and emotional devastation that terrorized people in every country, he continued, "This resurrection is proof that life is more powerful than death, that love is greater than hate, that good is more powerful than evil, and that truth is superior to vanity."

Since resurrection of the Lord Jesus Christ happened on the third day of His burial, the number three now holds great importance and meaning. The pope spoke of this in his homily.

Love Drives Out Fear and Restores Joy

They say that a person's life is three days: the day of birth, the day of death, and in between both is one long day called "the day of life" and a long day of life characterizes the [features] of human life...life containing many things but I want to concentrate on one point today about a person's life that is constrained by many fears. "The Lord is my light and my salvation; whom shall I fear? The Lord is the strength of my life; of whom shall I be afraid?" (Psalm 27: 1-2)

The pope went on to say,

A person stands perplexed before many fears that confront him in his long day of life and he may sometimes stand before God and ask, "Lord, where are you in the midst of all these fears?" Other times he may have the thought, "Lord, have You forgotten Your creation? The human you created with Your own Hands!"... Resurrection enabled man to cross over from a state of fear to a state of love... Resurrection transformed many people from living in fear into perfect state of love... Resurrection transforms man to live in his restored human state which is joy.

Pope Tawadros then spoke about "three steps we find illustrated in the glorious scenes witnessed in the events of the resurrection."

The First Step Is the Purity State

> It is impossible for a person to enjoy resurrection
> and be transformed from a state of fear to a state
> of love except by being in state of purity. I mean
> purity of heart. For a person to live life before
> God and be on the right path, as God intended,
> a person as God's creation must take this step of
> purity as it is written, "Blessed are the pure in
> heart, for they shall see God." (Matt. 5:8)

The pope then referred to the apostle Peter's denial of Christ,
though he is a disciple and yet fell into this sin! How is it he denies
his master before a servant girl?

> And we wonder, even the Apostle Peter himself
> felt it was over for him, that he had been rejected
> and so he lived in a state of fear and distance
> from Christ. After the resurrection of the Lord
> Christ, Peter went back to his old trade as a fish-
> erman. Later on, while Peter was fishing along
> with a few other disciples, he saw Christ standing
> at the shore. Christ invited them to "come and
> eat breakfast. (John 21:12)

So they did, and in the midst of this gathering Christ called the
apostle Peter who had denied Him and asked, "Peter, do you love Me"
(John 21:15)? The pope continues, "Three time the Lord asks Peter
the question and Peter answered the question and repeated his answer
once, twice, and three times, he told Christ, 'Yes, Lord you know that
I love you.' It was at this moment that Peter was transformed from a
state of fear to the state of perfect love, because he purified his heart
and his heart had become filled with love of the Master."

From that moment on, Peter became an evangelist and preached
in many places and many countries, and his life ended in martyrdom.
Pope Tawadros added, that the step of purity is the first step to lead

the person from a state of fear to a state of love. The one who lives in this love will never fear.

The Second Step Is Hope

"We know that hope and faith are very closely related. The person who lives in fear always has negative thoughts, and inhibiting thoughts can lead a person to some difficult situations in life that lead to hopelessness or even suicide. Hope is a critical step if a person is to move from a state of fear to a state of love."

The pope then reflected on Mary Magdalen as "the greatest example" of a disciple of Jesus. According to the Gospel accounts, Jesus cleansed her of seven demons. She was one of the witnesses of the crucifixion and burial of Jesus and was the first person to see Him after the resurrection. "She went to the tomb hopeful, driven by a powerful hope despite all the fear, the tears, and all the questions that must have been on her mind," the pope said.

Then he added,

> Beloved one, you who live in many fears, you must keep hope alive within you. So long as your faith is strong and as long you abide in the joy of the glorious resurrection, [this] will help you with any fears you may have until it brings you to a state of perfect love. The life of the person who lives in perfect love will be a very joyous one.
>
> This is why when we pray, we always say to Christ, "You are the hope of those who have no hope, You are the help of those who have no help." Lord, You are our Hope, and through the resurrection You have transformed fear and despair into joy and hope.

With regard to the second step of hope, the pope remarked there are people who are pessimistic and who see the worst aspects of things or believe the worst will happen, which leaves them in a state of despair versus "another person whose words make you feel that they always have hope for the future. He sees the good and believes that tomorrow will be better than today."

The Third Step Is Building

The pope explains building: "I mean taking action. A person who builds, he starts from the ground up. He works and so this is a step of ascension, of increase, of growth. If a person has taken the steps of purity and hope, then he will be active and productive." The pope reflected on Thomas, who doubted the resurrection of the Lord Christ. One week later, the Lord appeared again and said to Thomas, "Reach your finger here, and look at My hands; and reach your hands here and put it into My side. Do not be unbelieving, but believing. And Thomas answered and said to Him, 'My Lord and My God'" (John 20:27–28).

The pope then raised a question:

> And what did you do after that, Thomas? Well, can you imagine that Thomas moved from Jerusalem and went all the way to the other side of the world, to India, to preach the Name of Christ! That was an action step. If a person attains purity of heart and mind of hope, he will be able to build, he will be able to work, he will be able to embrace others and serve them. He will be able to transform from a state of fear to a state of love, and this is something that will bring joy to life.

Pope Tawadros II concluded his homily by stating, "Resurrection is not merely a celebration, nor is it merely a historical event. Resurrection is *life. Live it.* As we are in our homes today as families celebrating the glorious Feast of Resurrection, each one of us rejoicing and members of the family rejoicing with one another."[48]

Chapter Eleven

HISTORY MADE: QUEEN ELIZABETH SPEAKS ON EASTER

May the living flame of the Easter hope be a
steady guide as we face the future.
—Queen Elizabeth II

Queen Elizabeth II of the United Kingdom and fifteen other Commonwealth realms made an address to the public ahead of Easter Sunday. On April 11, 2020, *Daily Mail* royal editor Rebecca English reported that this was the queen's first-ever Easter speech in her sixty-eight years on the throne. She was keen to do so because of the special circumstances due to coronavirus and because traditional church worship would not be possible. The queen is head of the Church of England and "has a deep personal faith," says English.

The coronavirus led the queen to provide a special message on Easter out of care and concern for people around the world. She joined many leaders who pledged their support not only for their countries but also to all people around the world. As mentioned before, Pope Francis spoke of "the contagion of hope," acknowledging that for many, "this is an Easter of solitude lived amid the sorrow and hardship that the pandemic is causing, from physical suffering to economic difficulties."

Wanting to renew their faith and restore their hope, the pope asked, "Who will roll away the stone?" He then likens the stone that sealed the tomb of Jesus to the tombstones of the pandemic that "threatens to bury all hope" for the elderly living in isolation, for families who lack food, and for public-safety and health-care workers on the front lines who are "exhausted and overwhelmed." But the hope he offered to overcome coronavirus pandemic is the glorious resurrection of the Lord Jesus Christ and victory of life over death.

Alongside these dignified and noble thoughts, Queen Elizabeth offered similar words of hope, saying the "good news of Christ's resurrection has been passed on from the first Easter by every generation until now." She continued, "The discovery of the risen Christ on the first Easter Day gave his followers new hope and fresh purpose, and we can all take heart from this." She acknowledged that "this year, Easter will be different for many of us, but by keeping apart, we keep others safe. But Easter isn't cancelled; indeed, we need Easter as much as ever."

The queen added, "We know that coronavirus will not overcome us. As dark as death can be, particularly for those suffering with grief—light and life are greater. May the living flame of the Easter hope be a steady guide as we face the future. I wish everyone of all faiths and denominations a blessed Easter."[49]

Similar to Pope Francis and Queen Elizabeth II, Pope Tawadros II in his Easter homily began by acknowledging the pandemic's impact on the year's celebration for people around the world. "Yet this year we celebrate in a spiritual way with our families and in our homes, [not in churches] and this is wonderful," the pope said, assuring his audience not to fear the physical and emotional devastation of the pandemic and encouraging them to stand firm and be hopeful. Then he said, "This resurrection is proof that life is more powerful than death, that love is greater than hate, that good is more powerful than evil, and that truth is superior to vanity."

In Conclusion

It is only by divine providence that these three spiritual leaders—along with others not mentioned here—were inspired to deliver messages of spiritual awakening. When a world that exalts conquest in technological and scientific fields suddenly found itself facing an invisible and unknown virus, three holy and distinguished leaders in the East and the West joined forces to deliver an inspiring message of peace, love, and hope, thus trusting that the present and the future are subject to the inspiration and guidance of the Holy Spirit.

Though they spoke individually during the celebration of Easter, Her Majesty the queen of the United Kingdom and the popes of the Roman Catholic Church and Coptic Orthodox Church delivered empathetic and touching messages of wisdom, understanding, and hope reflected in the joyous and victorious meaning of resurrection's power: the risen Christ manifesting His present and future glory in us (Phil. 3:10–11).

Chapter Twelve

LEAVING AND CLEAVING

*To leave and cleave, and both become one flesh, how is it
considered marriage when he has abandoned his wife?*
—Pope Tawadros II

Covenant Marriage

Covenant marriage is a legally distinct kind of marriage for Copts
living in Egypt and in three American states (Arizona, Arkansas,
and Louisiana). In all these states, the marrying couples agree to
obtain premarital counseling and accept more limited grounds for
seeking divorce later. The Coptic Church does not allow for divorce
but will give a permit for remarriage as an exception due to special
circumstances (e.g., adultery or lengthy abandonment). For Copts,
both spouses may be granted such permit after a designated regional
Coptic Orthodox Council for Marital Affairs headed by the diocese
bishop reviews the case and makes a decision authorizing the party
that—in the committee's view—is not at fault to remarry.

Leaving and cleaving is a divine covenant and a fundamental
part of marriage's foundation. Why then is it an unkept promise
nowadays? We find couples who often fail to leave and cleave. At the
start, the newly married couple might not realize potential for stress,
anxiety, and even hurt caused by in-law interference and other problems. For this very reason, God has established specific boundaries
that should be carefully observed. The Lord says that a man shall
leave his father and mother and cleave to his wife, and they become

one flesh (Gen. 2:24). Parents no longer have authority or responsibility to run their children's lives. Married children need to pursue their lives independently and have the authority to lead their lives in the fear of God.

While children are expected to love their parents and never stop honoring them, God's plan is for married couples to establish emotional and financial independence when they marry, thus starting a new domestic church in their home. By continuing to depend on, consult, and seek the support of parents, newlyweds are not observing God's covenant to leave and cleave. One or both of the married couple will find it hard to cleave and be emotionally and physically intimate. For some reason, some parents find it hard to let go of the relationship with their daughter or son after marriage. Regretfully, they take pleasure in being "guardians" or protector of their adult child.

In-Laws Intrusiveness

Whether it's the husband or wife who is subjected to this intrusive relation of the in-law, he or she will feel offended, disrespected, and resentful. If it continues, marital relations will gradually deteriorate and conflict will flare up. One or both of the spouses will feel greatly disturbed and threatened by the presence of the in-law in their life. Surely some parental intervention is appropriate and should be welcomed. It is persistent intervention that children do not ask for that is destructive. That is because the children are not given the opportunity to achieve autonomy. Couple have to be left alone to focus on building their relationship, deal with problems themselves, and learn and grow together. Only then will they be able to appreciate each other develop and enhance their harmonious life. Otherwise the covenant of leaving and cleaving as intended begins to cool off and loosens to the point where one or both find it hard, if not impossible, to cleave.

The Truth Behind Splits!

When a loving relationship does not endure, the inevitable question arises: Is it time to split? Sadly, the divorce rate in the United States tells us that about 50 percent of all married couples at some point decide to break up.[50] Even with professional help, it may be too late if a damaged relationship had wiped out even a glimpse of hope after decades of trying to no avail. One of the spouses at least will be in a state of revolt and hopelessness. Women who usually bear the heavy burden of keeping the family together grow weary and depressed. They have done everything possible, including seeking professional help. They feel victimized by a husband who refuses to seek counseling and joining in to save his wife and family. As caring mothers, they try to protect themselves and their children. So they leave to save the tattered remnants of physical, emotional, and spiritual health and well-being.

Often lacking maturity and having a diminished sense of responsibly, spouses (mostly men) are unwilling to seek professional help. They are either ashamed or find it demeaning to meet with a third party to reveal their "limitations" or admit a failure to take good care of their spouse and family. The other spouse (usually a woman in this case) finds it hard if not impossible to carry on under these circumstances. They feel "this is as good as it's going to get." In many cases their men abruptly stop attending marital and/or family therapy sessions, while women continue for support and to learn to cope with the complex and difficult situation at home.

Many Christian couples turn to pastoral counseling and support. They usually are hopeful that the church will have great influence on the men to maintain a decent family life. They also engage the church in their unresolved and unsettled marital situations in the hope that it will have the final say should men be unwilling to abandon their distracted or abandonment behaviors. In many cultures, tough, stoic men and their lack of emotional expression is a hallmark of traditional masculinity. In addition, when it comes to Coptic men, countless husbands can barely show expressions of romance toward their spouses in public. It is especially rare among newly immigrated generations.

In clinical cases of marital therapy, men tend to complain that they work hard for up to twelve hours a day or even engage in more than one job to support the family and make ends meet. The reality is, in most clinical cases we find the husband is either a workaholic or feels "married to their jobs" or their coworkers. Having what is known as a "pseudo-wife" or "pseudo-husband" at work makes them happier at their place of employment than at home with their family. In such a relationship, there is no choice left for the homebound spouse but to leave, for there is no cleaving anymore, and there is no hope for the working spouse if he refuses to seek professional help or show the willingness to change.

Pope Tawadros II's View

On Marriage and Spousal Abandonment

In an interview with the official Coptic Orthodox TV station (CTV) broadcasting in Arabic to viewers in Egypt and many parts of the world, His Holiness Pope Tawadros II has much to say about Coptic Christian marital relations. In a program titled *House on the Rock* broadcast on July 31, 2020, he addressed spousal abandonment, saying, "The Bible tells us a man shall leave his father and mother and join to his wife, and they shall become one flesh… To leave and cleave, and both become one flesh, how is it considered marriage when he has abandoned his wife? The fulfilling presence is not there, marital covenant is not there. One has broken this covenant. Where is this marriage in the absence from the wife?

"Love is an art of making the other happy, and art needs time… Art means totality of feeling, and there is no selfishness. It is the renewal of their marriage; she would take a week vacation and he would do the same. A week by themselves to renew the marriage, it is not a routine. And family means, '*Father and Mother, I love you.*' Christ lives in the home… As we always say, homes of prayers, sanctified homes, blessed homes."

He then added,

> Both partners are to live in the fear of the Lord, for it is spiritual unity, thought unity, emotional unity, social unity and physical unity. In the absence of this unity, how this could be "leave and cleave"?…God wants this unity, 'Be fruitful and multiply; fill the earth' [Genesis 1:28], the family is the source of first love. The woman, her care is her husband, the woman is the center pole of the tent; the head is the man, which means the wise leadership; the head does not mean supremacy and domination [but] care and shepherding, empathy and service.

The pope also reflected on marital and personal affairs with regard to the current law of divorce. He said, "Lately the Christian churches [the three major Christian denominations] have come to an agreement with regard to what is known in the country as 'personal-status' law, the rules governing marriage, divorce, and inheritance for Christians in Egypt. The final draft of unified law is now awaiting the approval [of the state.]" For according to the faith and doctrine of the Catholic Church, there is no divorce, but it is possible to annul a marriage. However, in the Orthodox and Evangelical churches, divorce is possible but only under certain terms and conditions.

When the host of *House on the Rock* asked why marriages have become difficult and more complex than ever before, His Holiness responded, "The life of the family today with its vast changes is not the same as it was forty years ago." Viewing previous laws of 2008 and 2016, one could attest that during these earlier years the law of divorce was more lenient and less strict than the current ones. The pope spoke about spouses who abandon their life partner for three years or more will be considered for a permission to remarry. If they have children, they would need to have been away from the family for five years before being granted the permission to remarry. The pope, however, and understandably, did not reveal the history and causes of why this issue among Copts has worsened in recent years. Therefore, it behooves us to briefly review the historical facts about changes in church law regarding divorce starting in the past century.

The Coptic Church historically depended on a regulation called the 1938 Regulation, which permitted divorce in the case of seven situations: physical abuse, debauchery (i.e., extreme indulgence in bodily pleasures and especially sexual pleasure), persistence of aversion (i.e., strong feeling of dislike, abhorrence, horror), absence, imprisonment, infectious disease, and insanity.

In 2008, Pope Shenouda III approved amendments to the church's Personal Status Law, prohibiting Copts from divorcing except in two cases. The first was if the husband or the wife committed the act of adultery (only with substantiated evidence), which can be hard to prove in most cases. The second was if one of the two parties has changed religion. The Egyptian newspaper *Al-Ahram* wrote in March 2008:

> Things changed radically after Shenouda III ascended to the Coptic Papacy. He promptly rejected divorce on any grounds except adultery and extremely cruel treatment. Divorce and remarriage are only permitted for the innocent party in cases of adultery or conversion although this is currently a controversial issue after Egypt's Higher Civil Court ruled that Copts who had been through a civil divorce had the legal right to remarry.[51]

This ruling put the Coptic Church in a difficult position, as refusing to sanction divorces meant it was above Egyptian law. In the end, the Supreme Constitutional Court overruled the verdict and kept the status quo.

Pope Shenouda as a spiritual leader and a great defender of the faith defended his position. He stood firm not to accept any changes. In fact, during the controversy with Egypt's court ruling, he affirmed what was amended. In one of his popular and well-attended

Wednesday meeting in Cairo, he declared, "We respect the law, but we stand by the higher authority of the Bible." Then added, when it comes to such issues "I stand like a lion." The pope's response was based on the basic belief that the Coptic Church is a sacramental church, recognizing that the life of the Orthodox Christian is a mystical one grounded in the Holy Mysteries (sacraments), of which marriage is one.

The late pope, who experienced loss of his mother as an infant, knew well the importance of the presence of loving parents in the children's life. Protecting children from the devastating effect of divorce and nurturing the precious parent-child bond was clearly his solemn duty and the mission behind this fierce defense of 2008 amendment. Sadly, though, we live in an age of a "fatherless generation." A majority of fathers spend most of their time outside the home, causing what is known as "emotional vacancy." This impacts the boys' masculinity and has left mothers and daughters in tears, all retreating into the world of technology, where they can surf the internet endlessly to fill a bottomless vacuum.

Chapter Thirteen

LENS OF LOVE CONSTANTLY CHANGING!

*The best and most beautiful things in this world cannot be
seen or even heard, But must be felt with the heart.*
—Helen Keller

Marriage Is Honorable

Christians strive to be an example to those around them. Regretfully,
nowadays Christians seem to be following the lead of the world. It is
time to denounce many practices. It is the time to put love first and
sex back into its proper place. What is the proper place? It is within
the sanctity of marital relation, and "marriage is honorable among
all, and the bed undefiled; but fornicators and adulterers God will
judge" (Heb. 13:4). So what exactly is God's design for marriage?
Simply stated, His plan was revealed when he created Adam and Eve
and joined them together in the first marriage.

In Genesis 2:24, God says, "Therefore a man shall leave his
father and mother and be joined to his wife, and they shall become
one flesh." When Christians marry, it is important that both leave
their parents, meaning forsaking dependence on them for livelihood
and emotional support and depending on each other instead. Later
Jesus addressed marriage more precisely when He said, "So then,
they are no longer two but one flesh. Therefore what God has joined
together, let not man separate" (Matt. 19:6). No mother, no father,

179

and no in-laws should divide a couple who had made a covenant with each other, to leave, cleave, and become one flesh. Though we know that some parental intervention is appropriate, chronic intrusiveness by in-laws disturbs and even greatly threatens the relationship.

The married couple from the start needs to focus the lens of love on their life with each other through their relationship with the Lord. Their oneness means to shield themselves from any intrusive relationships and always examine whether they are enabling the thwarting of their own oneness and harmony by remaining dependent on parents and in-laws for support and care. The more married couple are unable to wean themselves from their parents, the more difficult it gets to leave and cleave. However, weaning means passage from one relationship to another, not a loss or detachment from a relationship. When couples appear helpless or dysfunctional unable or unwilling to strive for emotional healthy dependence, the more likely parents or in-laws feel obligated to interfere to provide support or even to save the marriage.

Lens of Love with No Light No Sight

First and foremost is the commitment of both to grow spiritually. Married couples gain strength and wisdom that leads to becoming one flesh. In marriage, their spirits become enlightened, ushering them gradually into unity of thought, concord, and closeness. Through the lens of love that must adjust its focus, newly married couples must learn to view all life through their oneness of "we" and "us" rather than the self-centeredness of an "I, me, myself" attitude. So when we speak of oneness, it means in the first place the oneness of the spirit. When the Bible says that man shall leave and be joined to his wife and the two shall become on flesh (Mark 10:8), the unity of flesh does not just happen, because becoming one flesh is a gradual and steady process.

Husband and wife both will grow intellectually, socially, and emotionally as they learn to share their deepest thoughts and feelings. Eventually, this process contributes to them growing in physical intimacy, culminating and fulfilling the oneness of body and soul.

The couple must recognize they need God or else their relationship will be doomed to fail regardless of how much love they may have for each other. For in the absence of divine light, there will be no sight to lead the married couple into the path of righteousness and conjugal love. The Lord makes the first move toward us, and He stirs up within us a desire and a thirst for Him and for one another. In this regard St. Pseudo-Macarius says, "If someone loves God, God's love is united with that person. If someone believes in God, God instils faith into him. So there is two-ways movement…From that moment onward you can do everything in sincerity and purity."[52]

Why Do Christian Marriage Fail?

It is a sad fact that marriages do fail, though God created and ordained the union. However, the institution of marriage is not the problem and is still the best possible relationship for a man and a woman to enter into. It requires effort to maintain and revitalize happy marriages. Every day, month by month, and year after year, wise couples, instead of taking the other spouse for granted, are proactive in keeping their warm relationship alive and well. Every good marriage maintains a commitment to a Christian relationship that is a lifelong choice with unconditional love, securely and happily sustained.

Identifying the following common reasons for marriages to fail does not mean that marriage itself does not work. Most marriages we saw over the years in clinical practice worked well, and therapy was instrumental in putting people's lives and families together. It has been our belief that marriage is a wonderful institution that is worth fighting for.

Lack of Commitment!

Both spouses know deep in their hearts that their marriage is built on the rock of their Savior. Their marriage is a spiritual, emotional, and physical, bond created by the triune God alone. As such, within the security of the relationship, marriage and family can grow and thrive. Regretfully, the lens of love occasionally changes and instead of prioritizing the relationship, it focuses on worldly distractions and physical attractions outside the bond of marriage. These distractions, if they persist, tend to cause the pledge of commitment to one another to disintegrate.

Quite often and usually early in a marriage, couples face disagreement or unnecessary conflict due to miscommunication or unreasonable or different expectations, then ignore or disregard and fail to resolve the issue. Problems then become increasingly toxic, and one or both spouses start to feel helpless. If they continue to be unwilling to restore their unity and harmony, both may drift apart or go through periods of distance using the blame game. Therefore, it is very important for couples to take proactive steps toward restoring harmony in the household before things escalate.

Loneliness and Abandonment!

Healthy marital relations provide the joy of companionship, a sense of belonging, and a shield of security that flourish with spousal trust. When companionship and warm feelings of unity and joy dissipate and there is an absence of romantic love and intimacy, relationships evaporate. Loneliness and sadness will dwell in the heart of the spouse who keeps looking to fill a void. Companionship is what keeps marriages sailing smoothly, bringing joy with something as simple as looking forward to returning home early rather than working late. There is a kindled desire to be with your spouse and your family and be closer rather than drift apart, thus deepening love for one another.

Communication Barriers

Another significant factor in failed marriages is lack of communication or communication barriers between the married couple. The art of communication and learning to understand each other is a lifelong challenge, and it is not just the words one uses but tone of voice, body language, and tender looks, warmth, and attentive listening. Some people may find it difficult to express their emotions due to lack of attention, competing interests, or distractions (TV on or iPhone pinging). When there is a lingering serious issue that feels important to address, both partners should find the appropriate time and place to talk. Communication should not be forced; a willingness to have this conversation is essential to resolve the issue. Another factor is to stay on topic without bringing past incidents into the present discussion to prove a point. Each spouse should try to be considerate of the other partner's feelings and be willing to listen, compromise, and be loving.

Lack of Physical Intimacy

There are times when a lack of physical intimacy may be a cause for deep concern, as presented by clients in clinical practice. Christian couples may even threaten divorce if the issue is not addressed. Men usually seems to have a higher libido than women, and this can cause issues in the relationship. While men can find treatment to perform the marital act, women do not have such a pill as a "libido booster," at least not yet. There are women who claim they have a strong drive or higher libido than their spouses, though it's less common.

Women are much more concerned about keeping their partner happy and are more willing to seek counselling than their husbands. Physical intimacy usually is based on complex interactions of many factors that include physical and emotional well-being as well as experiences and expectations of each person. This issue should be openly and sincerely addressed, and when needed, seeking professional medical and/or psychological help is quite beneficial.

Compulsive Watching of Porn

Watching pornography is one of many unhealthy behaviors and can cause extreme harm to marriages as well as to the ones who watch porn. Pornography is often portrayed as acceptable in our culture. Many newly married couples might argue that using pornography in marriage is stimulating and can "kindle the desire." However, watching pornography has extensive harmful effects regardless of one's age. It negatively impacts the intimate relationship in marriages. It certainly sacrifices spousal intimacy, and real, warm, and loving relations are abandoned. Most importantly, a husband damages his calling as a man to be a protector and a mature giver, another Christ to his wife and children.

The man who watches porn enters a virtual reality, allowing for more "intimate" and "personal" experiences in a fantasy world devoid of a true loving and intimate relationship. This is really about using another person for one's own personal pleasure. It damages the watcher ability to see the beauty and goodness of his wife and of marital love, sexuality, and chastity. It makes sex nothing more than a recreational activity and takes away the relational and procreative aspects of it, so nothing good can come out of it.

Some Christian societies consider pornography as a ground for divorce. Their concept is broad when they apply porn to the words of Jesus. They quote Him regarding "lust for her [another woman] has committed adultery with her in his heart" (Matt. 5:28). In this case, pornography—in their view—is equated with extramarital sexual activity, which violates the sanctity of marriage.

Lack of Purpose in Life

Marriages also fail due to lack of mission and vision, mainly God's plan for both lives together that goes beyond one's own desires, needs, and dreams. The true mission of a Christian couple is to know the Lord intimately and love Him with all heart, soul, and mind and love one's neighbor for the sake of His love. The faithful mission in life ought to surpass any other goal and be instrumental in extending His kingdom on earth as it is in heaven, to serve Him by seeking and saving souls here on earth and be with Him in the hereafter.

Declining Professional Counseling

No matter how much marriage thrives, there are times when conflict breaks down the relationship or couples face overwhelming problems and one or both spouses refuse to address their issues with professional counseling. Most likely it's an unhealthy ego standing in the way—in practice we usually find the husband is ashamed or embarrassed about seeking assistance. Seeking wise and godly counseling can surely save a marriage before problems intensify and become worse.

St. John Chrysostom, reflecting on marriage and conjugal rights, explains:

> St. Paul says: "The husband should give to his wife her conjugal rights, and likewise the wife to her husband." What "rights" is Paul speaking of?
>
> If a harlot tries to seduce you, you ought to think: "I am not the owner of my body; it belongs to another." And if the wife should think the same if anyone assails her chastity: "My body is no longer mine, it is my husband's." So that applies to both. Both of them have the same "rights." There are no special privileges for the man. "The husband does not rule over his own body, but the wife does." Perfect equality, no privilege.[53]

Chapter Fourteen

ONE GLORIOUS EASTER FOR ALL

Christ, our Passover, was sacrificed for us. Therefore let us keep the feast.
—1 Corinthians 5:7–8

Easter of 2020

Easter this year comes in the midst of the global coronavirus pandemic. Like all people across the world, Christians are living under various restrictions and self-isolation. Lent and the Pascha week preceding the great celebration of Jesus's resurrection on Easter Sunday is the most significant and sacred season for Copts and the entire Christian world. This year, the Orthodox Easter was on Sunday, April 19. Although Eastern Orthodox churches celebrate Easter on a different day than the Western churches, at rare times the dates coincide.

The celebration of Easter is traditionally a time for family and church gatherings. This year, Christians had to adjust to the circumstances due to coronavirus and have been creative in the ways they observe Easter. This included refraining from traveling and gathering in groups, streaming online church services, and making maximum use of social media to exchange greetings and visit with each other virtually.

Why Two Easters?

Easter is celebrated by one Christian faith but on two different dates, or what may be called the inconsistency of two Easters. It has remained a thorny problem for the Christian church. According to the World Council of Churches, "It has long been recognized that to celebrate this fundamental aspect of the Christian faith on different dates gives a divided witness and compromises the churches' credibility and effectiveness in bringing the Gospel to the world." The methodology used to set the date of Easter is identical for both Western and Orthodox Easters: the first Sunday after the first full moon (this occurs when Earth is located between the sun and the moon) when on or after the vernal equinox (two moments in the year when the sun is exactly above the equator and day and night are equal length).

However, the churches base the dates on different calendars: Western churches use the Gregorian calendar, the standard calendar for much of the world, and Orthodox churches use the older Julian calendar. The Coptic Orthodox Church's emphasis is on honoring tradition and keeping the history and identity of the church intact. In this context, many traditional theologians think that changing the rules governing its most important religious holiday may change the dates of scriptural readings for Christmas and Easter. To them, the change would chisel away at the foundations of an already besieged religious heritage.

The Coptic Church on Six Continents

Since the middle of the twentieth century, the Coptic Church has no longer been restricted to its original boundaries in Egypt. She became a global church, and the Coptic community at large has earnestly prayed and urgently pressed for one glorious Easter for all. The Coptic Church now has millions of her members living in every part of the world. They hope their compassionate mother church will be more understanding of families with different circumstances. Those who live outside Egypt, especially in the Western Hemisphere, have different holy day calendars in schools and at work. They are also subject to severe impacts of climate change, including snow storms and hurricanes. These unpredictable weather episodes may prevent any church from holding worship services, including holy day celebrations, at a moment's notice.

Last-minute cancelation of major holiday celebrations happened during Christmas and at other times in both the United States and Canada. These severe weather realities are here to stay, and the church has a major role in finding an overdue solution for her members in these countries and elsewhere to fully participate in worship and celebrations of major feasts.

The Holy Spirit to Guide the Holy Church

Copts of all generations miss attending these celebrations and sacred occasions. We all trust that the Coptic Church, guided by the Holy Spirit, will find a way to accommodate the urgent needs of her children wherever they are. The apostles and the Church Fathers met many obstacles and were capable of finding solutions. Their main mission was to serve and minister to the needs of the people in every culture wherever they went. Their goal was to proclaim the salvific message of our Lord and to seek and save souls. In courage and sacrificial love, they met with resistance and obstacles, but it did not sway them. The Fathers of the Church were determined to enlighten and guide the flock and not deprive the faithful from having an active part in the life of the church.

Although there are many differences within the broader Christian community, they do not rise to the level where our beliefs and biblical faith deviate significantly. The Coptic Orthodox Church is driven by patristic exegesis, the way Fathers of the Church constructed and interpreted biblical texts. The sources of the tradition are Holy Scripture, liturgical life, the creed and canons of the ecumenical councils, the writings of the Church Fathers, and the lives of saints.

True, it has been said that "East is East, and West is West, and never the twain shall meet" because these parts of the world differ in history, religion, political systems, and so on. Despite the obvious differences between East and West, Christians of open mind and good faith are able to deal with the complexity of this issue. Both civilizations shape their lives according to their religious beliefs. They possess the art of communication and are capable of understanding what may set them apart. You find each willing to compromise and resolve their differences without sacrificing their own core principles. Both respect and appreciate the differences in each other's spiritual beliefs and traditions, recognizing it is a crucial part of their civilizations.

Generally speaking, the major difference between Eastern and Western culture is that people in the East are more conservative and traditional than the general population in the West. But that does not mean the level of deviation extends to what each considers to be the "true faith" and what has been practiced and received through the history of the church in both the East and West. The key to address this topic has to do with our understanding of the essentials of the Christian faith. We can draw vivid boundaries around our faith based on the essentials that have been handed down to us through the Church Fathers. Anything we received and is still being practiced is legitimately our "handed down" faith. Anything that is outside these boundaries is not. However, within every belief system, in addition to essentials, there are nonessentials. These may be considered practices that do not affect whether a person belongs to the faith.

Reconciling East and West

The World Council of Churches (WCC) organized a meeting in Aleppo, Syria, on March 5–10, 1997. A meeting for reconciling the Eastern and Western calendars was proposed and was favorable to both sides. The methods for calculating the equinox—the twice yearly day on which the sun crosses the celestial equator when day and night are of equal length (around September 22 and March 20)—and the paschal full moon would be replaced with the most advanced, astronomically accurate calculations available. However, the WCC felt that astronomical observations depend on a precise position on earth as the point of reference. It concluded that it was appropriate to employ the meridian of Jerusalem, the site of Christ's passion and resurrection, as this necessary point of reference for the calculation of the March equinox and the subsequent full moon.

Pinning Down a Movable Easter

Since the beginning of the twentieth century, a proposal to change Easter to a fixed holiday rather than a movable one has been widely circulated, and in 1963 the Second Vatican Council agreed, provided a consensus could be reached among all Christian churches. The second Sunday in April was suggested as the most likely date.

The ecumenical council held at Nicea in AD 325 determined that Easter/Pascha should be celebrated on the Sunday following the first vernal full moon. Originally, Passover was celebrated on the first full moon after the March equinox, but in the third century the day of the feast came to be calculated by some Jewish communities without reference to the equinox, thus causing Passover to be celebrated twice in some solar years. The Council of Nicaea tried to avoid this by linking the principles for the dating of Easter/Pascha to the norms for the calculation of Passover during Jesus's lifetime.

The Council of Nicaea's decisions are expressive of the desire for unity. The council's aim was to establish principles, based on the scriptural data concerning the association of the passion and resurrection of Christ with the Passover, that would encourage a single annual observance of Easter/Pascha by all the churches. By fostering unity in this way, the council also demonstrated its concern for the mission of the church in the world. It was aware that disunity in such a central matter was a cause of scandal.

The WCC addressed the issue at its meeting in Aleppo:

> Despite differences in the method of calculation, the principles of calculation in the churches of both East and West are based on the norms set forth at Nicea [*sic*]. This fact is of great significance. In the present divided situation, any decision by one church or group of churches to move away from these norms would only increase the difficulty of resolving outstanding differences.[54]
>
> The Council of Nicea also has an enduring lesson for Christians today in its willingness

make use of contemporary science in calculating the date of Easter. While the council sought to advance the concrete unity of the churches, it did not itself undertake a detailed regulation of the Easter calculation. Instead it expected the churches to employ the most exact science of the day for calculating the necessary astronomical data (the March equinox and the full moon).[55]

The recommendation made by WCC, as stated in its meeting on March 1997, will have some different implications for the churches of East and West as they seek a renewed faithfulness to Nicaea. Both will face the need for education of their faithful. For Eastern churches, changes in the actual dating of Easter/Pascha will be more perceptible than for the Western churches. Given the contexts in which these churches live, this will require both patience and tact. For Western churches, on the other hand, the challenge may lie in communicating deeper aspects of the Nicene principles for the calculation of Easter/Pascha and in acquainting their faithful with the concerns and insights of the Eastern churches.[56]

Pope of Alexandria Honorable Mention

His Holiness Pope Tawadros II is the 118th pope of Alexandria and patriarch of the See of St. Mark. The pope has been known for his pragmatism, wit, and unflappability and wants to set the church on a new path to act proactively instead of reactively. His Holiness uses a big vision as the basis for what the church ought to do. He is motivating Copts to use long-term thinking to create lasting benefits for the church in the twenty-first century.

In 2016, Roman Catholic officials and Coptic leaders started exploring steps toward mutual recognition of baptism rituals and pilgrimage sites and reconciling liturgical calendars. To reconcile his church with the Vatican, His Holiness Pope Tawadros appointed the highly regarded theologian His Grace Bishop Epiphanius, who was also the abbot of St. Macarius Monastery, to spearhead a delegation for this purpose. Regretfully, in July 2018, the efforts came to a temporarily halt as HG Bishop Epiphanius was killed. Two men who were charged in his death and claimed to be monks with links to a group called "the Faith Protectors" who are vehemently opposed to changing the dates of Christmas and Easter.[57]

During the pope's official visit to Canada in September 2014, the subject of celebrating Christmas on the twenty-fifth of December was brought up by members of the congregations. Coptic families in Canada voiced their deep concern that if they were not allowed to do so, they no longer would be able to celebrate the most important church feasts together with their children and loved ones. This was because Coptic Church holy days did not coincide with school breaks, nor did they meet Canadian statutory standards for holidays to take off and celebrate with the family. Consequently, younger Coptic families especially were missing out on fellowship with peers and friends. Their own societal culture couldn't safeguard them from the madness of secular holiday celebrations. It is a fact that Copts honor and maintain beliefs, moral values, traditions, language, and proper conduct held in common with their family and friends when they are within the bosom of the church liturgical life. Also, we cannot underestimate the church's role in guiding her youth in leisure-time pursuits that impact many aspects of their behavior. It is customary for family members and friends to exchange gifts, enjoy a special festive meal, and join in special church services.

Upon hearing these concerns, the pope imparted his empathy and wisdom as a visionary who understands and is always willing to favor the spiritual needs of the Coptic community. He welcomed their wishes to celebrate Christmas on December 25 as an additional day of celebration. The Coptic Church would be willing to adopt its congregants' request for the sake and convenience of all worshipers. Pope Tawadros II always sees something beautiful in accommodating the expansion of spiritual services when the need calls for it.

Pope Tawadros II stated that the church through its history has expanded worship service from once a week to every day of the week. In fact, addressing his audiences in his weekly meeting in Egypt in January 2020, he said that the church used to celebrate Holy Liturgy on Sundays only. Then it added Fridays when it became the official rest day in Egypt. Then it included Wednesdays. His Holiness then said, "Now we celebrate the Holy Liturgy every day of the week." These were necessary changes made to accommodate the needs of the people for the benefit of their spiritual life.

At the same time, he reprimanded some of the Coptic extremist who appointed themselves as "protector of the faith" and who dared to oppose celebrating Christmas as an added service. A special celebration on December 25 was authorized by His Eminence Metropolitan Serapion after consultation with the pope of Alexandria to accommodate worshipers who, due to their special circumstances, couldn't attend Christmas celebration on January 7.

HE Metropolitan Serapion's Historical Move

HE Metropolitan Serapion celebrated for the first time "an added" Christmas celebration on December 25, 2019, in addition to the Christmas that would be celebrated on January 7 at the Holy Transfiguration American Coptic Orthodox Church in Chino Hills, California. Metropolitan Serapion started his speech to the congregation by saying, "Merry Christmas and happy new year soon." He then focused on the authority of the church not only to keep the faith intact but also as an institution that cares to meet the needs of the people. His Eminence illustrated the concept by comparing it to what the priest does to guide a confessor. As the priest guides a penitent's spiritual life, he acts as a wise physician to lead him or her gradually in a life of prayer and fasting. In this case, even the diocese's bishop would not intervene in the priest's role for spiritual guidance. The priest may limit the number of daily prayers to two instead of the seven found in *The Agpeya: The Coptic Prayer Book of the Seven Hours*. The priest may instruct the confessor to start practicing his fast twice a week only (Wednesday and Friday) instead the entire Advent fast. The same applies at the level of the diocese, where the bishop organizes his parishes that are each overseen by a priest and looks to meet the needs of his parishioners. This is also in accordance with the Holy Synod, being the highest authority in the church and in charge of formulating the rules and regulations regarding matters of faith and order of service.

HE Metropolitan Serapion differentiated between exceptions and change. Exceptions are those that can be handled in the moment, whereas change is about "the goal of change"—the goal is the salvation of the people. But change must also have point, for there is good change and bad change. Good changes must achieve two things. First, it has to be good for the spiritual life of the people, not just to help them in the moment. Second, the source of change must be examined for validity, including supporting evidence from church history in instituting the change.

As an example, consider what happened in the case of the Feast of Nativity and the Feast of Epiphany in the early church. Both were celebrated as one feast on January 6 (Julian calendar = Coptic month Tobe 11), called the Feast of Epiphany. In the East, a separate feast for the Nativity on December 25 (Julian calendar = Coptic month Kioahk 29) was introduced around the fifth century. The twenty-fifth is an issue in the land of immigration, and ignoring it is not helping the matter. Generations of Copts outside of Egypt want to know about the celebration of this Christmas feast. Many families have the flexibility where they work, and they can attend the traditional Christmas celebration on its designated dated in the Coptic calendar.

However, the December 25 date is for certain people who cannot attend the traditional date, and that is when we say it is an exception for them who have the need. We are very grateful for the support of HH Pope Tawadros II, who cared for this people, as well as for the priests who make it their mission to follow suit for the salvation of souls.

Metropolitan Serapion—the first hierarch and bishop of the Coptic Orthodox Diocese of Los Angeles, Southern California, and Hawaii—continues:

> We came here to stay... We are here to stay not to be foreign body but to be integrated into the society, to be real salt of the earth and the light of the world. That is why the church through [the] centuries always look at the society and also in

this society there is a fight between Christians and secular forces regarding Christmas.

So we reclaim Christmas as a Christian feast, not just a season of holidays. We have to fight back against all these secular [matters] and we ask as Copts not to be on the side of these secular forces attacking Christians. This is not the right side of history. While we keep our tradition, we also [join] with all Christians forces in the [United States] society, who are fighting that the twenty-fifth is a Christian feast, not a secular feast.

God bless this day and all the days coming until we have the additional two feasts, God willing, on the seventh and the eighth and the birth of Christ is our joy every day.

Chapter Fifteen

THE EXCELLENCE OF PARENTAL DISCIPLINE

In an earlier chapter regarding biblical discipline, we stated that the scriptures are our primary resource for raising physical, emotional, and spiritual healthy children. Parents are to follow the word of the Lord when raising their children. "Behold children are a heritage from the Lord, the fruit of the womb is His reward" (Ps. 127:3). It is the Lord's instructions for parent to "train up a child in the way he should go; and when he is old he will not depart from it" (Prov. 22:6). Older children also need to learn from parents as they compassionately explain to their younger siblings not to disregard or resent their parents' discipline. Let them understand only "a fool despises his father's instruction, but whoever heeds reproof is prudent" (Prov. 15:5).

Parents, though, have to remember a key factor in communicating with their children—"it is not what you say, it is how you say it." In other words, communication with the child has to be free from yelling and threatening. Anger and aggressive behavior are unacceptable because it impacts children with fear, anxiety, and resentment toward the parent. Both parents have to call each other's attention to it if one or the other behaves inappropriately or exerts harsh discipline. Otherwise, they are making the child feel insecure, and it could indirectly encourage manipulation tactics or lying out of fear and/or lack of courage to face an angry parent. As parents, be careful not to let your children's emotions drive you. Listen to their feelings so they know that you care, but stick to your biblical principles.

Discipline and guidance are not only the father's responsibility but also the mother's. Both of them should teach their children diligently. "Hear, my son, your father's instruction, and do not forsake the law of your mother, for they will be a graceful ornament on your head and chains about your neck" (Prov. 1:8–9). While parents carry this awesome responsibility, the Bible warn fathers, "Do not provoke your children to wrath, but bring them up in training and admonition of the Lord" (1 Eph. 6:4). Christian parents are reminded if they act accordingly, they will reap the benefit of a pleasant home life free from conflict, disobedience, and disrespect. As the Bible says, "Correct your son, and he will give you rest; Yes, he will give you delight to your soul" (Prov. 29:17).

In the meantime, parents must teach their children what the Lord says to them, "Children, obey your parents in all things, for this is well pleasing to the Lord" (Col. 3:20). However, parents and children should make it part of their daily life to study the Bible knowing that "all Scripture is given by inspiration of God, and is profitable for doctrine, for reproof, for correction, for instruction in righteousness, that the man of God maybe complete, thoroughly equipped for every good work" (2 Tim. 3:16–17). The fruits of such daily biblical study is actually part of the life of the domestic church.

All biblical teaching is essential to train the child from early childhood. Children are worthy gifts that each parent not only should be grateful to have but also should invest in their talents. The rewards are magnificent, as the Lord speaks to the children in Ephesians 6:1–3: "Children, obey your parents in the Lord, for this is right. 'Honor your father and mother,' which is the first commandment with promise: 'that it may go well with you and that you may live long on the earth.'"

Praxis of Exemplary Parental Discipline

Parental Righteousness

The following account of Zacharias and Elizabeth is a shining practical model for Christian parents to emulate. Both parents are indeed "followers of God as dear children" (Eph. 5:1), and the story shows how "the Lord shows compassion to those who fear Him" (Ps. 103:13). John's parent not only fear the Lord but also, as the scripture describes, Zacharias and Elizabeth "were both righteous before God, walking in all the commandments and ordinances of the Lord blameless" (Luke 1:6). No greater compliment could be paid to John and his parents than the testimony of our Lord: "Assuredly, I say to you, among those born of women there has not risen anyone greater than John the Baptist" (Matt. 11:11).

Family Prayer Life

The first step for parents is to practice prayer life. The family that prays together stays together. With prayer life comes the fruits of righteousness and living blameless in the eyes of the Lord, as we have seen with Zacharias the priest and his wife. After so many years of unanswered prayers, they continued that righteous path surrendering to God's will and His plan.

One day, the angel of the Lord delivered the long-awaited answer to both parents' prayers. The angel said to Zacharias:

> Your prayer is heard; and your wife Elizabeth will bear you a son, and you shall call his name John. And you will have joy and gladness, and many will rejoice at his birth. For he will be great in the sight of the Lord, and shall drink neither wine nor strong drink. He will also be filled with the Holy Spirit, even from his mother's womb. (Luke 1:13–15)

Caring parents, let us pause and reflect on God's amazing gift to both Zacharias and Elizabeth. A son, John, was the fruit of long and fervent parental prayers, a unique baby gifted with unheard-of physical and spiritual credentials, for he was great in the sight of the Lord before his birth; John was filled with the Holy Spirit even from his mother's womb.

Parents, do you fear your children may get involved in drinking and drugs? Let us then learn from John's righteous parents. Parental prayers over the years bestowed the gift of God to John. He was shielded from such habits or negative influences, for he "shall drink neither wine nor strong drink." Considering nowadays the poisonous environment of schools and social media, parents ought to talk to their adolescent children as they are exposed to alcohol and other drugs. Parents have a significant influence on their children's decisions to experiment with these substances, but this can only happen if the parents are maintaining a strong, open relationship, a nurturing family, and a prayerful life.

That is surely what prayers will do when a mother conceives a baby and both parents pray for the gift of a righteous child. Thus both must "seek the Lord and his strength; seek His face evermore!" (1 Chron. 16:11). Planned or unplanned pregnancy, boy or girl, healthy or frail, each child has his or her own gift; parents then can say with the righteous Hannah, "For this child I prayed, and the Lord has granted me my petition which I asked Him" (1 Sam. 1:27). Whatever gifts parents receive from the Lord's hand, gratefully thank Him and bless His name, trusting in what He says "that all things work together for good to those who love God, to those who are called according to His purpose" (Rom. 8:28).

Do Not Plan the Child's Vocation!

John's parent did not plan his vocation; the Lord did. He says, "Before I formed you in the womb I knew you; Before you were born I sanctified you" (Jer. 1:5). Parents will do well to refrain from planning their children's career. They can discover their gifts, nourishes their growth, guide them in their education, motivate them to excel

199

in what they study, mentor them, and support and encourage them to cultivate virtues, pursue positive habits, be involved in physical exercise, and read books for intellectual stimulation and growth. All these activities are of utmost importance.

Both parents need to spend quality time with their children, especially in early childhood. They should read books to them and provide educational toys that will leave positive impressions on their brain well into their late teens. A two-decade-long research study has shown that the more mental stimulation a child gets around the age of four, the more developed the parts of their brains dedicated to language and cognition will be in the decades ahead.[58]

Parental Influence

John's parents brought up a humble, simple, ascetic hermit and a prophet. John the Baptist was a man of deep humility. The nature of his task kept him in the spotlight. As recorded in John 1:19–28, the religious leaders of Jerusalem and John wanted him to speak of himself, but he could speak only of the Messiah. When he was asked, "Who are you?" he confessed, "I am not the Christ." John openly encouraged his disciples (one of whom was Andrew) to leave him and follow Jesus (John 1:37). When others tried to stir up jealousy due to the popularity of Jesus, John indicated that he was privileged to draw the attention to Christ and not himself. In his words, "He must increase, but I must decrease" (John 3:30) and, "The Father loves the Son, and has given all things into His hand" (John 3:35).

If we examine the Bible carefully, we can trace John's humility and ascetic life to his parents, Zacharias and Elizabeth. St. Luke tells us in his Gospel (Luke 1:39–44) that Mary arose and went into the hill country with haste to the city of Judah, and she entered the house of Zacharias and greeted Elizabeth. When Elizabeth heard Mary's greeting, the baby leaped in her womb, and Elizabeth was filled with the Holy Spirit. Then she spoke out with a loud voice, "Blessed are you among women, and blessed is the fruit of your womb! But why is this granted to me that the mother of my Lord should come to me?" A picture of total humility!

Like his mother, John was a humble man, but he was also an ascetic hermit. One of the most unique features of John was his apparel. Camel's hair garment and leather belts were not the attire of the fashionable young men of Jerusalem. He would not accept food from others; he ate only locusts and wild honey (Matt. 3:4). His appearance had a specific purpose: Zacharias had been told that his son would go forth in the spirit and power of the prophet Elijah (Luke 1:17). Elijah was described as "a hairy man and wore a leather belt around his waist" (2 Kings 1:8).

John's attire was designed to associate him with Elijah and his ministry. John could not be wearing fine cloth while preaching that true repentance should result in compassion for the needs of others. Jesus testified to his simplicity and ascetic life when He said to the multitude concerning John, "What did you go out to see? A man clothed in soft garments? Indeed, those who wear soft clothing are in kings' houses" (Matt. 11:8).

John grew up with this mental image that he should have the spirit and the power of Elijah, and he was raised accordingly. He dressed like the prophet and knew that he had a ministry to fulfill just as Elijah did. Who do we think planted this promise in his memory while growing up? No doubt it was his parents.

The question now is, Do we practice the same when we baptize our children? Baptism gives us new life as adopted children of God. Our children are usually carrying a saint's name or given one when baptized. Raising the child to adopt the same characteristics of the saint he or she was named after helps the child to mature in goodness. Through the practice of virtues, such as the cardinal virtues (prudence, justice, temperance, and fortitude), our children will grow to honor God in whatever they do to the glory of His name.

Parents ought to learn from John's saintly parents and see to it that the child knows in depth the life story of his or her patron saint—how the saint "fought the good fight, finished the race, and kept the faith" (2 Tim. 4:7). The saint whose name is chosen for the child at the time of baptism will serve as a special patron to protect, guide, and be a heavenly intercessor for them. The child, supported by parental love, care, and support, studies the life of the saint and keeps a picture as a model to emulate and to celebrate his or her victorious and saintly life.

And while we are at it, we should always remind our children that the best gift that they ever had and will ever have is their baptismal event. They became children of God and a member of His Body of Christ. The kingdom of God is theirs if they remain faithful to Him and observe His commandments.

In his homily during the celebration of the Holy Theophany of Our Lord and (January 18, 2013), His Holiness Pope Tawadros II beautifully illustrated a magnificent concept. He quoted from the Old Testament, "For dust you are, and to dust you shall return" (Gen. 3:19). But after baptism, he said, "We are from heaven and to heaven we shall return, as we are no longer old creation but anew." What a beautiful, joyful, and uplifting reality so sweetly uttered by the Coptic pope of Alexandria!

Chapter Sixteen

THE FAMILY BETWEEN FAITH AND CULTURE

So now faith, hope, and love abide, these three,
but the greatest of these is love.
—1 Corinthians 13:13

A happy family is but an earlier heaven.
—George Bernard Shaw

The Family

Our Heavenly Father's plan of salvation is to enable us to become like Him and receive a fullness of joy. By divine providence, baby Jesus chose to be born and grow up in the Holy Family of Joseph and Mary. Not only that, but His church is nothing other than a family of God. However, families suffer in these troubling times, for the world is quite hostile to faith and faithful people. The family is burden with huge responsibilities indeed. As it has been said that raising children nowadays is a "mission impossible."

Parents find it quite difficult most of the time to instruct their children in the faith while competing with the distractions and destructive images of the digital world. But the most drastic causes of Christian family failures today come from within, and in our clinical experience, the person most responsible for that is the husband and father. He is to be the head of the family and the captain of the ship, yet he ignores or gives up on these responsibilities. With the excuse of work and stress or ambition to achieve his own objectives in life, he leaves this responsibility to the wife. Jim George, a bestselling author who dedicated his writings to helping people live a life after God's own heart, sums up this tragedy in the following words:

> The Christian family is under attack on all fronts. Christian marriages are disintegrating at an alarming rate. Children are not receiving the proper training and modeling from the Christian parents. And, from my perspective, a major contributor to this tragic slide is usually a husband and father who is not fully assuming his God-ordained role as a spiritual leader.[59]

The Domestic Church

Raising godly children is quite a challenge to say the least. Though parents are still the primary instructors of the faith, they are hardly able to do it. But by God's grace, if they are invested and willing, they can. It is a well-known fact that the Christian family is considered the "domestic church." The term dates all the way back to first century AD. The phrase *ecclesiola in ecclesia* (Latin: "little churches within the church" refers to this. Our early Church Fathers understood that the home was fertile ground for discipleship, sanctifications, and holiness. Within the domestic church, parents are to cultivate a family life that is centered on Christ. Christian believers are quite conscious of the importance of family, dignity, and the role of parents!

All who care about the meaning and the theology of the domestic church ought to expand this passion for the unique role that God has in mind for our lives and the lives of our family members. One of the documents of the Second Vatican Council, *Lumen Gentium* (Latin for "light of the nations"), illuminates this concept. The home is the secure place and protective environment where baptized children learn about their faith. The document states, "From the wedlock of Christians there comes the family, in which new citizens of human society are born, who by the grace of the Holy Spirit received in baptism are made children of God, thus perpetuating the people of God through the centuries.[60]

It Takes a Village to Raise a Child

Raising a faithful child is not the responsibility of the parochial schools or the Sunday schools. Both may affirm what the parents teach, but parents ought to lead by their word and example, being the first preachers of the faith to their children. They should encourage them to build their lives in fear of the Lord as well as help them discover gifts endowed to them by their Creator that leads them to live spiritual and successful lives. The core family, with the help of other supportive family members, including the church family, shapes the child spiritually from his or her earliest days. They provide their first school in Christian living and lead them to the gift of a spiritual and successful life.

True, it takes a village to raise a child, but most importantly, it will take a firm marital commitment between the parents to remain faithful to each other. Through their love, support of one another, and active participation in the faith, as well as their commitment to raise their children with a love for Christ and His church, they can do it. The children will indeed turn out to be the salt of the earth and His radiating light, witnessing to all they meet along the path of life. The domestic church will remain forever the first place where young children experience the empowering unity, the bonding, strength, and the shining light of living the faith in their own lives and the lives of those who cross their path.

Family Values and Societal Culture

The terms "family values" and "traditional values" have become synonymous in the United States and imply a congruence with mainstream Christianity. However, today's culture in the States tends to challenge faith in our homes, schools, and places of work. Cultures of industrialized countries have shifted from traditional to secular values. The presence of the digital world and the rise of knowledge-based economies has caused countries to shift from values of survival to values of self-expression. Many of traditional families have become concerned about the challenges their children are confronted with. Their children openly contest many well-established family values and traditional thinking from their upbringing.

New generations are subjected to contemporary American culture that includes both conservative and liberal elements. They debate scientific and religious competitiveness, moral values, materialism, and free expression. Regretfully, these heated discussions have ignited during this election year (2020), with people attacking each other's political ideologies and positions. Many are unwilling to engage in political discussion or express their point of view, especially in academia or even at home with family. Yet only an open, robust environment for free speech will support the quest for truth. Parents should discuss any challenges children face in school or in the community at large and debate these matters at home. Parents who welcome their children's cultural or political views can still help them build understanding and enlighten their views, thus helping them to lead a more mature, God-fearing life.

Even if the topics at time seem contradictory to one's believe or traditional thinking, it is important to keep an open mind. It is essential to hear what the other party has to say as long as the matter is discussed politely and respectfully. After all, children are growing and still learning, but parents may need to be open to fresh ideas as well. The essential role for parents, however, is to build the spiritual life of their children as they grow and devote time for the family to pray together. John C. Broger, an American author and a Christian missionary, once said, "In addition to teaching your children throughout the day, you must set aside specific, planned times to worship the Lord and His words together. Conducting family devotions requires planning and diligence if this godly practice is to develop and be maintained in your home."

Ways to Build a Culture of Hope and Love

More than ever, Christians should be well versed in reasons for believing and compassionately engage with opposing points of view. We should not remove ourselves from sharing our faith with non-Christians. Be ready to give the reason for our hope even when some criticize our faith. We can show love and tolerance to the unbeliever even when they decline to show us the same courtesy. After all, this what true Christianity is all about. In a culture that has lost hope, the faithful's hope goes beyond materialistic gains and earthly desires. It is an unshakable confidence in God even when we face difficulties that give us every reason to doubt.

G. K. Chesterton observed that hope is meaningful only when things are hopeless. "As long as maters are really hopeful, hope is a mere flattery or platitude," he wrote. "It is only when everything is hopeless that hope begins to be a strength."

However, we as Christians cannot present ourselves to the world as hopeful, loving people unless we have cultivated early in life the theological virtues of faith, hope, and love. These virtues are related directly to God. They are the foundation of Christian moral behavior and are bestowed upon us as God's gift in baptism. So hope to a Christian is that we desire, and have full trust in and await from God, the kingdom of heaven and eternal life and the graces to merit it. It behooves Christian parents to teach their children the difference between our culture of hope as a virtue rooted in Christ and the worldly concept of hope.

Our hope is not mere worldly desires and wishful thinking—it is our faith in the Lord. Only through these heavenly gifts, clothed with humility, can we win this spiritual battle. Our hearts are always filled with hope even in the midst of family troubles, world hostility to faith, agonizing pain, and suffering. Christians especially should not fall prey to bouts of anxiety, hopelessness, depression, insecurity, and fear. With faith and hope, there is no need to turn to illicit drugs or alcohol to alleviate down moods or try to feel good, then suffer regrets and shame. Hope in the Lord brings encouragement and teaches us to patiently wait on the Lord and be at peace in His unfailing love for us.

"And hope does not put us to shame, because God's love has been poured into our hearts through the Holy Spirit who has been given to us" (Rom. 5:5).

The Unconditional Love and Truth

Love is the center, the summit, and the sublime element of Christian belief. It is the boundless love of Jesus Christ for humanity, the love of Christians for Christ, and the love of Christians for others. Our love for Christ is a reflection of His love for us. Love begins at home, cultivated and nourished within the life of a loving family. First it shines through the tender loving care between spouses. Children emulate this love as they witness it in parental relation. Parents lead by example and help children to know that God's love is not tied to performance, nor does He expect us to work harder to win His love. His love for us is unconditional.

The importance of love in the family can be summarized in the word of Pope Francis: "We learn many virtues in our Christian families. Above all, we learn to love, asking nothing in return... The Christian family is missionary: it announces the love of God to the world."

On the same subject, St. Thérèse of Lisieux writes in her autobiography *The Story of a Soul*:

> When the Lord commanded His people to love
> their neighbor as themselves, He had not as yet
> come upon the earth. Knowing the extent to
> which each one loved himself, He was not able
> to ask of His creatures a greater love than this for
> one's neighbor, but when Jesus gave His apostles
> a new commandment, His own commandment
> (John 15:12) as He calls it later on, it is no longer
> a question of loving one's neighbor as oneself but
> of loving him as He, Jesus, has loved him, and
> will love him to the consummation of the ages.[61]

Since our love is a response to Christ's unconditional love, we need to teach our children at home, within the church family, and in Sunday schools. We must also instill in them that love without the truth is a lie. The truth here is not something, it is somebody—it is Christ. He is the one and only truth to recognize and heed this biblical fact. In today's culture, our children will be taught that the truth is subjective—what you believe is true for you; what I believe is true for me. They are bombarded throughout their lives by many claims of truth from the digital world, friends, and peers in school or at work. If we are not seriously invested in our children early in life to teach them biblical principles, they will surely struggle to win the cultural battle, and some may adopt this kind of relativism.

Seeking the Truth

The following is the story of a young girl who was born into an observant Jewish family but had become an atheist by her teen-age years. Edith Stein (1891–1942) grew to be a brilliant philoso-pher, author, and teacher. She was awarded a doctorate in philosophy with summa cum laude. Stein became a member of the faculty at the University of Freiburg, where she worked until 1918. Through her many years of searching to find the truth, she came to know that Jesus was the ultimate truth she had been looking for. After reading the autobiography of the mystic St. Teresa of Ávila during summer holidays in Bad Bergzabern in 1921, Stein converted to Catholicism and eventually sought the life of a Discalced Carmelite.

On August 7, 1942, more than nine hundred Jews were deported to the Auschwitz concentration camp. It was probably on August 9 that Stein, now known as Sister Teresa Benedicta of the Cross, and her sister Rosa were killed in a mass gas chamber with many others.[62] Later, she was canonized as a martyr and saint.

St. Teresa Benedicta had reflected on the importance of truth and love during her life and beautifully integrated both. Jesus has these words for us: "Love your God with your whole heart, your whole soul and your whole mind; and love your neighbor as your-self" (Luke 10:27).

The words sound simple, but it is very hard to put them into action. We find that as we try to proclaim the truth, we do not do it with love. And when we tell someone we love them but we do not love them or fail to love them, this can lead to distrust and disappointment. That is what St. Teresa Benedicta found out, and she said, "Do not accept anything as the truth if it lacks love. And do not accept anything as love which lacks truth! One without the other becomes a destructive lie."

These biblical and objective realities are so essential while we live in a culture that is quite hostile to Christianity and even to the concept of God. When we proclaim truths without love, we turn people off and appear to judge them as if we know better than them, and we are perceived as self-righteous and judgmental. If or when we judge, we certainly do not love our neighbors as ourselves. Based on the Lord's commandments and church teaching, we find many of these truths seem to stand on their own merits. However, to proclaim them, we will be ignored or even laughed at, ridiculed, or disregarded as irrelevant.

For example, if we say abortion is wrong because the Bible says, "Thou shalt not kill" (Exod. 20:13), the gay lifestyle is unacceptable, and divorce and remarriage without an annulment is wrong, and we shouted out, "They all should be excommunicated," we are declaring these acts as truths without love. Thus, truth that lacks love is a destructive lie. As such, we appoint ourselves as judges, yet we are not called to judge others, for that is God's role. For instance, the Coptic Orthodox Church expresses doctrinal disapproval of abortion but offers forgiveness and healing to women who had abortion. The church shows them God's mercy by receiving them with open arms once they have confessed and repented, thus allowing them to resume partaking the Holy Communion as members of the body of Christ.

It is the same in the Catholic Church, where the late Pope John Paul II reached out to women who have had an abortion in his encyclical letter *Evangelium Vitae* (EV), the Gospel of Life. He shows compassionate understanding and gentleness of soul in supporting these women. While he affirms the church's stance on the issue as an "unspeakable crime," he acknowledges that the decision to have an abortion is often tragic and painful for the mother (EV, f8). This is what it means when we speak of sharing truths with love, for without love we fail in loving our neighbor as ourselves.[63]

Fundamental Change Is Needed

Change is difficult for everyone. Transformation via "renewal of the mind" as a path to solutions is impossible without taking into account the root causes of the problems. Without knowing what a person needs to change and if they are willing to act on it, he or she may remain content with the status quo. Societal change requires people to be collectively willing and ready to seek such change. Analyzing the culture determinants of societal problems may make it possible not only to understand causes but also to address them and find real, permanent solutions.

In addition, being able to explain clearly how changes are related to one's depth of knowledge and belief make things easier. That leads us not only to talk about building a culture of hope and love but also points to the determinant source of this sublime hope and unconditional love. We must strive to make it clear that love without truth should not be accepted because "one without the other becomes a destructive lie." That leads us to speak of another cardinal virtue, which is faith.

Determinants of Faith

Faith usually implies certitude even where is no evidence or proof. Faith is one of the three theological virtues, which are faith, hope, and love. "And now abide faith, hope, love, these three; but the greatest of these is love" (1 Cor. 13:13). For believers, "Faith is the theological virtue by which we believe in God and believe all that he has said and revealed to us, and that the Holy Church proposes for our belief, because he is truth itself."[64]

Speaking on faith and the importance of concerted and communal efforts of all, Pope Tawadros II had the following inspiring words in an interview with the Coptic television channel Logos TV, where he reflected on the importance of faith in the life of the four men who were instrumental in bringing the paralytic to Jesus.

> They worked in harmony together and were able
> to overcome every obstacle on the way until they
> reached where Jesus was. They removed the roof
> above Him; and when dug an opening, they let
> down the pallet on which the paralytic was lying
> right in front Him. His holiness said that the four
> men resemble the church, whose task it is to pres-
> ent sinners to Jesus. Each of the men is strong
> in his faith, and each of them is strongly needed
> to accomplish this task. They are the bishops,
> the priests, the deacons, and all the people. Each
> church member ought to resemble the four faith-
> ful men in the story of the paralytic

As we reflect on the pope's inspiring words, one realizes that we have been blind to more subversive cultural sins that have great impact on the church and are contrary to the kingdom. The message of the kingdom is a message of community where all belong to each other in eternal relationship. It appears that unknowingly, these sins may have been supported by many of us, and as members of the body of Christ we have faltered in our mission. One dares to say we are now inclined to think first about ourselves rather than having Jesus as the first priority. He is the most important truth, which behooves His followers to emulate His life with the gifts we have been given by serving one another and our neighbor.

With this solidarity among the bishops, the priests, the deacons and all the people, we all are charged with the responsibility to seek and save souls, because sin is an offence against God: "Against you and you alone, have I sinned; and I have what is evil in your sight" (Ps. 51:4). Moreover, sin gives rise to social norms and institutions that are contrary to the divine goodness. The expression "sinful social structure" describes the effect of personal sins. They lead their victims to do evil in their turn and tend to "grow stronger, spread, and become the source of other sins, and so influence people's behavior."[65]

Thus, this an inspiring call by Pope Tawadros II for all the faithful not only to proclaim the message of salvation and redemption but also be the good shepherd who leaves his flock of the ninety-nine sheep in order to find the one that is lost. We have to emulate the faith of the paralytic's friends, work together in harmony, and be able to overcome every obstacle on the way while searching for the stray sheep and recovering of the lost. We must also remember that the same applies to the domestic church and the spiritual health of its members. The head of the family is the priest. In fact, St. Augustine calls him the bishop of the family; the mother is the queen.

St. John Chrysostom says the husband is the head while the wife is the heart. Both are essential for life of the human body. The children are members of the family who must be cared for; you must invest in their physical, emotional, and spiritual well-being. Under the leadership of the Holy Spirit we taste His fruits. Under His leadership we seek the astray, and through fervent prayers the prodigal son or daughter will return home to the bosom of the Father.[66]

Let us always remember that today's attack is focused on the family. The evil one knows that destroying the family means the destruction of relationships and the moral fabric of the society of nations. The spiritual health and emotional stability of the family are the most important factors not only for the survival of the family today but also increasingly for the family to become salt of the earth and light of the world. Then and only then by faith, hope, and love can we impact people around us and transform cultural practices and cultural relativism toward a better life...the abundant life.

Prerequisite of Faith

As we spoke earlier about determinants of faith, we must now speak about prerequisites for faith to understand the doctrine of faith. Many speak of simple faith without studying the depth of its call to believe in God's promises and trust in His faithfulness, which leaves the person in a state of unripened faith. It is an advantage to have completed some study to be enlightened. "But solid food belongs to those are of full age, that is, those who by reason of use have their senses exercised to discern both good and evil" (Heb. 5:14). To explain this further, let us consider the writing of St. Clement of Alexandria:

> It is possible to be a faithful Christian without knowing how to read. But it is impossible to understand the doctrine of faith without having studied it. Accepting the right ideas, rejecting erroneous theses: this cannot be done by simple faith, but only by faith that has been ripened by scholarship...it is an advantage to have completed some study and to have one's faculties trained by practice.[67]

Chapter Seventeen

WHAT DO YOU WANT GOD TO DO FOR YOU?

When Jesus saw the man lying there who had been lame for thirty-eight years and knew he had been in that condition a long time, He said to him, "Do you want to be made well" (John 5:6)? Many have pondered Jesus's question. It seems incredible to ask a seriously ill person if he wants to get well. A definite "Yes!" seems like the obvious answer!

Why, then, did Jesus asks this question? The Lord possibly wanted to see if the man still had the desire or hope to get well. This sick man of Bethesda, after all those years, may have become despondent. How sad for him that of all the people who came to celebrate a religious festival, none would help him!

It seems that a devout person might have helped him to get into the water, but not even one would do so. However, he remained hopeful, because he most likely believed that one day he would walk healed and healthy as long as the pool's water was stirred by an angel (John 5:4). He had seen others who were blind, lame, and crippled recover and walked away. Had he lost hope or patience, he would have left the pool a long time ago. We also might consider the reason Jesus asks the question is to teach us it is important not to make assumptions but discern people's needs before we pray for them or provide help. When people ask for prayers, some respond humbly, "Saints' prayers be with you!" or "St. Mary, pray for us all!"

That is absolutely a worthy answer, because "the fervent prayer of a righteous person is very powerful" (James 5:16). Based on overwhelming evidence from scripture as well as the constant tradition of the Church, we can be assured that the saints in heaven can hear our prayers and are praying for us. Having said that, as laborers in the vineyard of the Lord, it behooves us not to assume that a person only wants a prayer; they may have a specific favor or request they want us to pray about. It is worth imitating Christ, to discern the will and the need of the person who requests a prayer, just as the Lord asked the man, "Do you want to be made well?" In fact, the one who requests such prayer would likely appreciate such respect and personal attention.

This pool was called in Hebrew "Bethesda," which means "house of mercy." But the lame man who had been there for thirty-eight years had received no mercy. In other words, the place was supposed to be a house of mercy, but it was not. This act of mercy was apparently what the paralytic was expecting! It is interesting to note that the solution to the man's problem was not the people or the religious activities; only Jesus could help him, but he couldn't see it. He was focused on getting to the pool. He wanted to use Jesus to help him get to the pool. He wasn't looking to Jesus for the healing itself.

When Jesus said to the sick man, "Do you want to be well?" he answered, "Sir, I have no one to put me in the pool when the water is stirred up; while on my way someone else gets down there before me" (John 5:7). Notice this man didn't even know who Jesus was, and so his faith was not involved. Therefore, we learn from the scriptures not only to discern people's needs when they ask us to pray for them but also to ask ourselves what we want God to do for us as we pray. Just like this man had used his resources for thirty-eight years to get well, we usually depend on our own resources or others to solve our problems. When they don't work, we despair, becoming disheartened and frustrated with ourselves or resentful of other people.

Sometimes we do turn to God, but with the wrong goal in mind. Just like this man who wanted Jesus to help him get down to the pool, I think we often look to God to give us what we think we need, when in fact what we need is God Himself. If someone is depressed about work or financial issues, he wants God to give him a better job to help him earn extra money rather than just depend on God and let Him work out the details. If a spouse is depressed over a bad marriage, he or she wants God to change the other person, when maybe the one that needs to change or at least learn to depend on God for the fulfillment that no human can possibly give.

"Rise, take up your bed, and walk" is the Lord's statement of healing (John 5:8). The important point for us is that when Jesus gives a command, He also enables us to carry out the command. If we see a command in scripture that we are to follow, we don't do it by our own power. We do it through the power that God supplies.

St. Evagrius of Pontus puts it squarely for us when he says, "Pray that the will of God may be done in everything. He, in fact, wants what is good and useful for your soul, while you are not always seeking that and only that."[68]

Fr. Domadius Anba Bishoy (1862-1950)

Chapter Eighteen

THE UNTOLD STORY OF A SAINTLY MONK

"No one can serve two masters: For you will hate one and love the other… You cannot serve both God and money."
—Luke 16:13

The untold story of Fr. Domadius Anba Bishoy is included here at the request of the monks of Anba Bishoy Monastery of Wadi El Natrun, Beheira Governorate, Egypt. They heard about Fr. Domadius's life through my book *The Exemplary Leadership of Pope Kyrillos VI & Pope Shenouda III*[69] and expressed their wish to add his biography to the monastery archive.

Fr. Domadius's story is valuable because it tells of the struggle of a wealthy man who realized that the riches of his present life were not his own but God's. He was only a steward employed for the good of men and the honor of God, who will reward or punish accordingly.

The story of this saintly monk is filled with tragedies, excruciating pain, and unbearable suffering. Unlike the story of Job, Fr. Domadius did not end up restoring his family life and regaining his tragic losses. But he trusted God's wisdom and plan. From the story of this righteous monk—from a life of prominence, prosperity, and happiness to a chain of sudden tragic events—we can learn of his virtues and gain insight into coping with pain and suffering.

Finally, I share his story for families today who suffer from losses of business, income, or precious lives. The coronavirus pandemic has had unprecedented widespread impacts on families across America and the world. It has raised concerns about our ability to weather long-term health and financial crises. Most importantly, the sudden death of loved ones has severely impacted family life and reduced its strength, especially when the death is of a parent and the children become motherless or fatherless. In this story, when the children realized they would never see their parent again, they became saddened and insecure. However, as you read, you will notice when God's grace intervened, the family was spared from emotional disturbance and saved from devastation and hopelessness.

The Life of Fr. Domadius

Throughout his life, tragic events had struck Fr. Domadius and his family repeatedly. The story of this saintly monk not only can help console families who suffer losses, it also encourages them to know about God's caring love, enabling them to endure tough times with great fortitude.

In the case of Fr. Domadius's family, rhythms might have shifted, but family ties remained as strong and loving as ever. His family found deeper meaning and more reward to live a life of faith, and they became resilient and able to stand strong and recover quickly from tragic events. They developed a deep understanding for heartache, learned empathy, and were compassionate toward their neighbors and those who crossed their path.

Fr. Domadius's Background

Fr. Domadius was born to wealthy and devout Christian parents. His father, Gabriel, and mother were childless for many years, but the merciful Lord answered their prayers and the wife conceived and gave birth to a son, who they named him Dawoud (David). They raised him in fear of the Lord and to love their church of St. Serapion, where they baptized their newly born son. Dawoud was a good and loving child since his youth. Later in life, his parents wanted him to get married and chose for him a young girl named

Demiana. She happened to be one of their relatives and was of similar social status. She was named after St. Demiana, who with the forty virgins were Coptic martyrs in the early forth century in Egypt.

Dawoud was not in favor of the idea, yet being obedient to his elderly parents, he married Demiana at a relatively young age. He was blessed by this marriage, and his new wife joined him and lived with his family. When his parents died, he inherited a farm of what was said to consist of seventy acres, famously known as the "Swidden farm." The farm carried this name until the revolutionary 1952 land-reform law for equitable land ownership. The farm was situated on a very fertile land in Malij or Melig, a village, three miles northwest of Shibin El-Kom, a city in Egypt's Nile Delta and the capital of Monufia Governorate.

Dawoud became a very prosperous person. Beside his farm, he owned a store selling gold jewelry and diamonds in Alexandria. Since he was the only child, his parents ever had, he considered having a larger family, believing children are a gift from God and a blessing. His wife gave birth to four healthy boys named Haleem, Gabriel, Messiha, and Morcos. No doubt having four children transformed the life of their parents and added to their blessings and responsibilities. Raising four children is not a small matter, and they became busier as the children grew older. The two older sons, as they came of age, helped their father on his farm and with his numerous business responsibilities while the two younger sons continued their education. All four children were raised to have strong faith and to honor their parents and respect their decisions.

Is Suffering Part of God's Plan?

Indeed, life for Dawoud's family was flourishing and seemed enriched with abundance. However, the good life did not last. The family was stricken by the tragic death of the two older children. One day, Haleem and Gabriel returned home sick after spending the whole day under the heat of the sun while working at the farm. Apparently, both suffered from heat exhaustion, and in the absence of prompt

221

medical attention, they became very sick. They never left their home again and within forty days died from heatstroke two weeks apart.

Their parents were in total shock. As many of us will do, most likely Dawoud asked the question: *"Why me?"*

He probably looked for a reason or some forgotten sin as the cause. According to both the younger sons, no one could understand this tragedy or explain why it happened. The community of the faithful tried to console the family, yet the parents were totally devastated, becoming withdrawn and secluded. In his deep grief, Dawoud may have fallen victim to the culture of the day and thought his suffering must have a traceable cause. If this was not enough, his beloved wife, Demiana, departed earthly life to join her older sons soon after.

Following the death of his wife, Messiha and Morcos said that their father's life came to a halt. He became subdued and could hardly leave his home, let alone go to his farm or attend to his business in Alexandria. The two younger children were finishing their education and were neither involved nor capable of managing the farm or the jewelry business. His struggle with intense grief lasted almost a year, but eventually he seemed at peace and was very supportive of his younger sons, expressing to them it was God's will and of the need to accept it and trust Him.

Dawoud's Resolution!

According to Morcos, their father explained to them their suffering may have a purpose. That purpose was not always punishment, although sin does bring punishment. But that was only a small part of suffering's role in the life of those who trust God. He said they all ought to continue praying and wait on the Lord and His plan for their lives.

One day, Dawoud called both sons to tell them some "dreadful" news—he had sold all his possessions and planned to go to the monastery of Anba Bishoy, where he would spend the rest of his life. He tried to ease the impact of this harsh news by teaching them that "money was the root of all evil" and that he had realized he could not serve both God and money. The only thing he left them was the family home.[70]

Both sons were saddened, and the younger one expressed his disapproval in tears, although he tried not say anything that might upset his grieved father. Later on, he voiced his disagreement over his father's untimely decision. It was not because Dawoud sold all his possessions or decided to spend the rest of his life in a monastery, but rather, he and his brother felt suddenly alone without any emotional or financial support. They had lost both of their older brothers in a very short time, then their loving mother. On the day their father confided his plan to them, they felt abandoned by him, the one and only support they had.

Dawoud afterward left to enter the Anba Bishoy Monastery. There he took the monastic vows and was ordained a monk, named Domadius Anba Bishoy in honor of St. Domadius, the son of King Phalintianus. He later was consecrated a priest and given the authority to administer all the sacraments of the church except the sacrament of ordination (which only bishops have the right to do).[71]

In later years, Fr. Domadius was elevated to the rank of hegomen (archpriest).

God's Plan Unfolded!

Messiha and Morcos moved to Cairo and resided there. Messiha joined the Egyptian military and later was honorably discharged after being deployed in Sudan for six months. At that time, Sudan had been united with Egypt for nearly 136 years, becoming an independent sovereign state on January 1, 1956. Following his discharge from service, Messiha started his civilian life and worked for Shell oil company in Cairo until retirement. He was married to Matelda, the daughter of a reputable Christian family from his own small town. Together they had a large family of five children.

In the meantime, Morcos moved up the ladder of his career and was the one and only Christian engineer appointed to oversee the large, ambitious projects of the Tahrir Directorate in Egypt.[72] The Tahrir Directorate was established under the leadership of President Gamal Abdel Nasser in the early 1950s. It became one of the largest agricultural centers in the world in production of fruit.[73] Morcos continued serving in this capacity, overseeing the megaprojects in the heart of Egypt's desert and staying there until retirement. He was truly a humble man who lived a monastic and celibate life even as an unmarried layman.[74]

Departure of the Saintly Monk

Fr. Domadius remained at the monastery of Anba Bishoy close to the end of his earthly life. After he had fallen sick and required special treatment, he left the monastery to be cared for by his older son's family. There he received comprehensive treatment, coordinated and supported by his loving family. Fr. Domadius was happy to be surrounded by his two sons and loving grandchildren once again. Daily he would bless them with his prayers and share with them inspiring stories and the treasures of the faith.

On Tuesday August 29, 1950, early in the morning, Fr. Domadius departed his earthly life to be with the Lord and was buried in the family tomb. His funeral procession was planned and honored by representative of Pope Yousab II of the Coptic Orthodox Church. The liturgical and funeral service was conducted at the Coptic Church of St. Barbra in Old Cairo, Egypt.

In Conclusion

I present *The Untold Story of a Saintly Monk* to the Anba Bishoy Monastery's archive, honoring their request for Fr. Domadius's biography. But more importantly, I also want to share it with the readers. Many families today have suffered from major losses of business, income, and lives due to the coronavirus pandemic. However, as we read the life of Fr. Domadius and his decedents, we know that God is truly in control. "And we know that all things work together for good to those who love God, to those who are called according to His purpose" (Rom. 8:28). Hopefully, the reader will see in the unfolding events of this true story that when God's grace intervened, the family was spared from emotional disturbance and saved from devastation and hopelessness. Fr. Domadius and his family had experienced immense suffering, but not only were they saved, protected, and loved, God also provided the means for members of the family—despite the tragedies that had befallen them—to feel secure and loved and continue to maintain a strong and positive bond. We also witnessed how they enjoyed each other's company and went on with their lives serving the Lord and seeking and saving souls to the glory of His name. It is worth noting that the oldest grandson of this saintly monk, Hegomen Domadius, was ordained a priest by the personal invitation and hands of HH Pope Shenouda III. And his great-grandson was ordained by the hands of HH Pope Tawadros II to serve the Coptic Orthodox Church abroad.

Redemptive Suffering

In *The Imitation of Christ*, it says:

> JESUS HAS always many who love His Heavenly Kingdom, but few who bear His cross. He has many who desire consolation, but few who care for trial. He finds many to share His table, but few to take part in His fasting. All desire to be happy with Him, few wish to suffer anything for Him. Many follow Him to the breaking of the bread, but few to the drinking of the chalice of His passion.[75]

For many who dread suffering, we are taught, and rightly so, that redemptive suffering is the Christian belief. Human suffering, when accepted and offered up in union with the passion of Christ, can remit the just punishment for one's sin, for the sins of another, or for the spiritual growth of oneself or another. "For to you it has been granted on behalf of Christ, not only to believe in Him, but also to suffer for His sake" (Phil. 1:29). Suffering alone without being united with Christ is a curse, and no one should bear it. But suffering with Him is temporary, and glory is eternal.

Appendix
AUTHOR'S QUOTED IN THE TEXT

Ambrose (339–397). Probably born in Treviri. Started a political career and became a governor. His seat was at Milan. Not yet baptized when he was elected bishop; he received baptism and consecration in the same week. He gave away his inheritance to the poor and dedicated his energies to listening, counseling, and helping everyone. He took a stand against various heresies, including Arianism. Ambrose was a pastor of souls as well as a scholar, with an eloquent, sometimes poetic style. Chief works: *Hexaemeron, On the Gospel of Luke, On the Holy Spirit, The Mysteries, Penitence.*

Augustine (354–430). Born in Thagaste, Tunisia. Augustine had an undisciplined youth, during which he fathered an illegitimate son. Despising the Christian faith of his mother, Monica, he joined the Manichees. He became a teacher of liberal arts and secured a position in rhetoric at the imperial court at Milan. There, listening to the sermons of Ambrose the bishop, assimilating the Neoplatonic philosophy of Plotinus, and reading the letters of St. Paul, he came back to Christianity. In the autumn of 386, Augustine gave up teaching, retired into the country, and was prepared for baptism, which Ambrose bestowed on him during the Easter Vigil of 387. For some years, he led a monastic life with friends. In 391 he was ordained priest; four years later he was consecrated auxiliary to the Bishop of Hippo, Valerius, and on his death inherited his See. Even as a bishop, Augustine continued to live in community. Tireless in the care of the poor, a forceful preacher, and a persuasive writer—his style is particularly evocative—Augustine was very involved in the theological controversies of the age. Besides his *Confessions,* some of his main writings were *The Soliloquies, The City of God, On the Trinity,* and commentaries on Genesis, the Psalms, and the Gospels.

Clement of Alexandria (Titus Flavius Clemens) (c. 150–c. 215) was a Christian theologian and philosopher who taught at the Catechetical School of Alexandria. A convert to Christianity, he was an educated man who was familiar with classical Greek philosophy and literature. As his three major works demonstrate, Clement was influenced by Hellenistic philosophy to a greater extent than any other Christian thinker of his time, and in particular by Plato and the Stoics. His secret works, which exist only in fragments, suggest that he was also familiar with pre-Christian Jewish esotericism and Gnosticism. In one of his works, he argued that Greek philosophy had its origin among non-Greeks, claiming that both Plato and Pythagoras were taught by Egyptian scholars. Among his pupils were Origen and Alexander of Jerusalem. Clement is usually regarded as a Church Father. He is venerated as a saint in Coptic Christianity, Eastern Catholicism, Ethiopian Christianity, and Anglicanism. The most important of his surviving works is a trilogy comprising the *Protreptikos* ("Exhortation"), the *Paidagōgos* ("The Instructor"), and the *Strōmateis* ("Miscellanies").

Cyril of Jerusalem (c. 315–386) was a distinguished theologian and archbishop of Jerusalem in the early church. In 381, he took part in the Council of Constantinople, famed for his twenty-four cat-echeses (preparation for baptism), the last five of which have particular importance for sacramental theology. He is venerated as a saint by the Roman Catholic Church, Eastern Orthodox Church, Oriental Orthodox Church, and the Anglican Communion. In 1883, Cyril was declared a Doctor of the Church by Pope Leo XIII. He is highly respected in the Palestinian Christian community.

Gregory of Nyssa (died 394). Younger brother of Basil. At first Gregory studied rhetoric and founded a family, but then, chiefly at the instigation of his friend Gregory Nazianzen, he retreated to the solitary life. Later, at the insistence of Basil, he agreed to become Bishop of Nyssa in Cappadocia. As bishop, he visited the churches of Pontus and eventually was named patriarch of Sebaste. He had remarkable speculative qualities. Chief works: *Major Catechetical Discourse, Against Eunomius, Dialogue on the Soul and Resurrection, The Creation of Man, The Life of Moses,* and homilies on the Song of Songs, Ecclesiastes, the Beatitudes, and the Lord's Prayer.

Evangrius of Pontus (346–399). Ordained deacon by Gregory Nazianzen, Evagrius attracted many followers in Constantinople through his eloquence. Realizing how much his inner life was at risk through his popularity, he left the city and went to live with monks in the mountains of Nitria. There he became a friend and a disciple of Macarius the Egyptian. He copied books for a livelihood. His thoughts owed much of their inspiration to Origen, whose works he tried to spread among his fellow monks. He is the first monk to develop a considerable literary legacy. Some of his works include *Gnostic Problem, On Prayer, Mirror for Monks, Mirror for Nuns,* and commentaries on the Psalms and Proverbs.

Isaac of Nineveth (c. 613–c. 700) also remembered as St. Isaac the Syrian and Abba Isaac. He was a seventh-century Church of the East Syriac Christian bishop and theologian best remembered for his written works on Christian asceticism. Because the administrative duties did not suit his retiring and ascetic temperament, he requested to abdicate after only five months and went south to the wilderness of Mount Matout. He was an important ascetical and mystical author. After many years of studying at the library attached to the monastery, he emerged as an authoritative figure in theology. Shortly after, he dedicated his life to monasticism and became involved in religious education throughout the Beth Qatarya region. Isaac is remembered for his spiritual homilies on the inner life, which have a human breadth and theological depth that transcends the Christianity of the church to which he belonged. They survive in Syriac manuscripts and in later Greek, Arabic, and Georgian translations; from Greek they were translated into Russian.

Irenaeus (died c. 202). Coming from Asia Minor, disciple of Polycarp, he was a priest in Lyon and then bishop of the same city. He showed himself to be skilled polemicist in confrontations with Gnosticism. On the other hand, when Pope Victor I excommunicated the churches of his native country, Irenaeus urged the pope to reestablish unity. According to a sixth-century historian, he died a martyr's death. Irenaeus wrote in Greek. From his many works there survive *Against Heresies* and *The Demonstration of the Apostolic Preaching.*

John Climacus (575–649). Monk on Mount Sinai, author of *Stairway to Paradise* in which he analyzes in thirty chapters (or steps) the vices that threaten monks and the virtues that distinguish them. In them he puts emphasis on tradition: anyone seeking orthodoxy should inquire into the teaching handed down to the apostles and living in the body of the church.

Maximus the Confessor (580–682). Belonging to a distinguished family in Constantinople, Maximus first became secretary of the emperor, then went into a monastery near Scutari. Fleeing from the Persians, he moved to Alexandria and possibly to Carthage. He held violent disputes with Monophysites and Monothelites. He persuaded some synods and eventually the Lateran Synod at Rome to condemn Monothelitism. He was taken as a prisoner to Constantinople and condemned to exile in Thrace. A second trial restricted him to Colchis after having his tongue cut out and his right hand amputated, the limb that symbolized commitment as "confessor," as a witness to the true faith. He died soon after as a result of the amputation. The most brilliant theologian of his time; he was concerned also with mystical, exegetical, and liturgical problems. His works are often hard to understand and written in a bombastic style.

Polycarp (69–155) was a Christian bishop of Smyrna. According to the *Martyrdom of Polycarp*, he died a martyr, bound and burned at the stake, then stabbed when the fire failed to consume his body. Polycarp is regarded as a saint and Church Father in the Eastern Orthodox, Oriental Orthodox, Catholic, Anglican, and Lutheran churches. His name means "much fruit" in Greek. Both Irenaeus and Tertullian record that Polycarp had been a disciple of John the Apostle. In *On Illustrious Men*, Jerome writes that Polycarp was a disciple of John and that John had ordained him Bishop of Smyrna. Polycarp is regarded as one of three chief Apostolic Fathers. His role was to authenticate orthodox teachings through his reputed connection with the apostle John.

Pseudo-Macarius (490–560). The greatest of the old Byzantine poets, Pseudo-Macarius exercised his priesthood in Constantinople. Although he composed a thousand hymns, only sixty-five extant ones are authenticated as his. Some have found their way into liturgical use. His hymns on the Nativity and on Easter are particularly impressive.

Theodoret (393–460). Born in Antioch, nominated, against his will, to the See of Cyrrhus. Even so, he performed his pastoral office with admirable zeal. Theodoret took an active part in the Christological controversy instigated by Nestorius. He is one of the most prolific authors of the Greek Church, and he wrote, for example, *The Exposition of the True Faith, Discourses on Providence, Cure of Pagan Diseases,* and commentaries on the Psalms, the Song of Songs, the Prophets, the Pauline epistles, and the history of the Church.

Notes

[1] Irenaeus, *Against Heresies*, 4, 25 (Harvey II, p. 184), God does not need us, But He Longs to Shower us with Gifts; Thomás Spidlík, *Drinking from the Hidden Fountain* (Cistercian Publications, Collegeville, MN: 1994), p. 27.

[2] Dorotheus of Gaza, Teachings, 5 (SC92, pp. 251ff), We need guidance on the way; Thomás Spidlík, *Drinking from the Hidden Fountain* (Collegeville, MN: Cistercian Publications, 1994), pp. 104–105.

[3] John Climacus: *Stairway to Paradise*, 21 (PG 88, 945) *Tackle Your Fears Head-On;* Thomás Spidlík, *Drinking from the Hidden fountain* (Collegeville, MN: Cistercian Publications, 1994), p. 144.

[4] Ibid.

[5] Diagnostic Criteria from DSM-5.

[6] UPI, "Reagan Phone Calls Spurned," *New York Times*, July 25, 1982, p. 26.

[7] Augustine, *Joy: An Uneasy Bedfellow,* Thomás Spidlík, *Drinking from the Hidden Fountain* (Collegeville, MN: Cistercian Publications, 1994), p. 46.

[8] Gregory of Nyssa, *On the Lord's Prayer,* 2 (PG44, 1141); Thomás Spidlík, *Drinking from the Hidden Fountain* (Collegeville, MN: Cistercian Publications, 1994), p. 345.

[9] Augustine, *Christ is the Gate that is Humble and Low, On the Gospel of John,* 45, 2 (PL35, 1720ff.); Thomás Spidlík, *Drinking from the Hidden Fountain* (Collegeville, MN: Cistercian Publications, 1994), p. 319.

[10] Maximus the Confessor, *Centuries on Charity,* 4, 63ff. (SC9, pp. 165ff.) *Neither Slaves of Passion nor too Strict in Mortification;* Thomás Spidlík, *Drinking from the Hidden Fountain* (Collegeville, MN: Cistercian Publications, 1994), p. 76.

[11] Thomas à Kempis, *The Imitation of Christ* (Mineola, NY: Dover Publications, 2003), p. 46.

[12] Ibid.

[13] Theodoret, *The Cure of Pagan Diseases,* I, 78 (SC57, 124), *As the Eye Needs Light;* Thomás Spidlík, *Drinking from the Hidden Fountain* (Collegeville, MN: Cistercian Publications, 1994), p. 377.

[14] Maximus the Confessor, *Mystagogia,* 6 (PG9I, 684), *Beyond the Husk of the Literal Sense;* Thomás Spidlík, *Drinking from the Hidden Fountain* (Collegeville, MN: Cistercian Publications, 1994), p. 380.

[15] Bishop Gregory, *Spiritual Values in the Sacrament of the Holy Eucharist* (Cairo, 1966,) p. 92.

16 A. J. Russell, ed., *God Calling: Your Loved Ones* (Uhrichsville, OH: Barbour Publishing, 1989) p. 6.

17 Clement of Alexandria, *Miscellaneous Studies*, 4, 22, 135ff. Stählin II, p. 308), *The Perfect Person's Rule of Life;* Thomás Spidlík, *Drinking from the Hidden Fountain* (Collegeville, MN: Cistercian Publications, 1994), p. 158.

18 Theodoret, *The Cure of Pagan Diseases*, 6, 74 ff (SC57, 281), *We Think of Him as Human, We Adore Him as God;* Thomás Spidlík, *Drinking from the Hidden Fountain* (Collegeville, MN: Cistercian Publications, 1994), p. 396.

19 Cyril of Jerusalem, *Catecheses*, 10, 1ff. (PG 53, 660), *The Door that Opens the Way to the Father;* Thomás Spidlík, *Drinking from the Hidden Fountain* (Collegeville, MN: Cistercian Publications, 1994), p. 393.

20 Thomas à Kempis, *The Imitation of Christ* (Mineola, NY: Dover Publications, 2003), p. 7.

21 Augustine, *Serm. Morin I, I (Miscellanea Agostiniana 447ff.) God Found a Harlot and Made Her a Virgin;* Thomás Spidlík, *Drinking from the Hidden Fountain* (Collegeville, MN: Cistercian Publications, 1994), pp. 316–317.

22 *Encyclopedia Britannica Online*, s.v., "St. Thomas Christian Apostle," accessed July 8, 2020.

23 Clarence W. Hall, "The Village That Lived by the Bible," *The Heartbeat of the Remnant*, Ephrata Ministries, Nov/Dec. 2005, ephrataministries.org, accessed July 8, 2020.

24 Augustine, *On the First Letter of John*, I, 4 (SC75, 121) *God is Light;* Thomás Spidlík, *Drinking from the Hidden Fountain* (Collegeville, MN: Cistercian Publications, 1994), p. 390.

25 Gregory of Nyssa, *The Creation of Man, 18 (PG44, 192), The Two Faces of the Human Race;* Thomás Spidlík, *Drinking from the Hidden Fountain* (Collegeville, MN: Cistercian Publications, 1994), p. 32.

26 Theodoret, *The Cure of Pagan Disease*, I, 90ff (SC57, 128) *Even Learning the Alphabet Needs Faith;* Thomás Spidlík, *Drinking from the Drinking from the Hidden Fountain* (Collegeville, MN: Cistercian Publications, 1994), p. 377.

27 Fr. Paolo O. Pirlo, *My First Book of Saints* (Parañaque City, Philippines: Sons of Holy Mary Immaculate—Quality Catholic Publications, 2014), pp. 58–59.

28 Ambrose, *On the Gospel of St. Luke, 7,* 124ff. (PL15, 1751); Thomás Spidlík, *Drinking from the Hidden Fountain* (Collegeville, MN: Cistercian Publications, 1994), pp. 154–155.

29 Cyril of Jerusalem, *Catecheses*, 4, 22ff. (PG33, 484); Thomás Spidlík, *Drinking from the Hidden Fountain* (Collegeville, MN: Cistercian Publications, 1994), p. 64.

30 Isaac of Nineveh, *philocalia, Continually Before the Face of God;* Thomás Spidlík, *Drinking from the Hidden Fountain* (Collegeville, MN: Cistercian Publications, 1994), p. 359.

31 Ibid.

32 Clement of Alexandria, *Miscellaneous Studies,* 6.2. (SC30, 71) *Scholarship Is a Help to Faith;* Thomás Spidlík, *Drinking from the Hidden Fountain* (Collegeville, MN: Cistercian Publications, 1994), p. 384.

33 Miguel Mary Fr., *Eternal World Television Network,* broadcasted November 2012.

34 Augustine, *De doctrina christiana,* II.xvi.23. R. P. H. Green, trans. *On Christian Teaching* (Oxford: Oxford University Press, 1999), p. 44.

35 Jeremy Hunt, *Foreign Secretary Report Order,* BBC News, May 3, 201936. Thomas à Kempis, *The Imitation of Christ* (Mineola, NY: Dover Publications, 2003), p. 63.

36 Ibid.

37 Augustine, *Confessions,* trans. Henry Chadwick (New York: Oxford University Press, 1991), p. 3.

38 Augustine, On Psalm 33, 9 (PL36, 313), *Do Not Seek Special Favours from the Lord*; Thomás Spidlík, *Drinking from the Hidden Fountain* (Collegeville, MN: Cistercian Publications, 1994), pp. 368–369.

39 Maximus the Confessor, *Centuries on Charity,* 4, 63ff. (pp. 16f55.); Thomás Spidlík, *Drinking from the Hidden Fountain* (Collegeville, MN: Cistercian Publications, 1994), p. 76.

40 Thomas à Kempis, *The Imitation of Christ* (Mineola, NY: Dover Publication, 2003), p. 58.

41 Haddon Robinson, *THANKS, Our Daily Bread,* RBC Ministries, GR, MI, March, 97.

42 Dorotheus of Gaza, *Teaching,* 3 (SC92, pp. 209ff) *Conscience, a Spark of Life*; Thomás Spidlík, *Drinking from the Hidden Fountain* (Collegeville, MN: Cistercian Publications, 1994), p. 93.

43 Lisa Miller, *The Spiritual Child: The New Science on Parenting and Life Long Thriving* (New York: St. Martin's Press, 2016), p. 52.

44 Thomas à Kempis, *The Imitation of Christ* (Mineola, NY: Dover Publications, 2003), p. 64.

45 Ibid., p. 32.

46 John Cardinal Krol, Cathedral of SS. Peter & Paul. Philadelphia, Pennsylvania, June 13, 1976.

47 Gerard O'Connell, "Pope Francis Shares His Vision for Covid-19 Aftermath," *America: The Jesuit Review,* April 17, 2020, https://www.americamagazine.org/faith/2020/04/17/pope-francis-shares-his-vision-covid-19-aftermath.

48 Pope Tawadros II, "Easter Homily on Resurrection," April 19, 2020, Monastery of Saint Bishoy, Wadi El Natrun, Egypt, translated to English by Dr. Esmat Gabriel.

49 Darcy Schild, "Queen Elizabeth II Said Easter 'Isn't Canceled,'" www.insider.com, April 11, 2020.

50 Chrisanna Northrup et al., *The Normal Bar* (New York: Harmony, 2013).

51 Al Ahram Newspaper, *Divorce in the Coptic Church,* March 2008.

52 Pseudo-Macarius, Homilies, 15, 20ff. (PG34, 589) *When Grace takes Passions of the Pastures of the Heart;* Thomás Spidlík, *Drinking from the Hidden Fountain* (Collegeville, MN: Cistercian Publications, 1994), p. 65.

53 John Chrysostom, *On the First Letter to the Corinthians,* 19, I (PG61) *My Body is no Longer Mine; It is My Wife's;* Thomás Spidlík, *Drinking from the Hidden Fountain* (Collegeville, MN: Cistercian Publications, 1994), pp. 197–198.

54 World Council of Churches/Middle East Council of Churches Consultation, *Towards a Common Date for Easter,* Aleppo, Syria, March 5–10, 1997.

55 Ibid.

56 Ibid.

57 Mina Nader and Jacob Wirtschafter, "Egypt's Coptic Christians Celebrate Christmas, Ponder Changing Date," *National Catholic Reporter,* December, 26, 2018, https://www.ncronline.org/news/world/egypts-coptic-christians-celebrate-christmas-ponder-changing-date.

58 Alok Jha, "Childhood Stimulation Key to Brain Development, Study Finds," *The Gurdian,* October 14, 2012.

59 Jim George, "Good Reads," https://www.goodreads.com/quotes, Topic 63.

60 The Second Ecumenical Council of the Vatican, *Dogmatic Constitution on the Church, Lumen Gentium,* §11; 11 October 1962–8 December 1965.

61 St. Thérèse of Lisieux, *Story of a Soul,* 3rd ed., (Washington, DC: ICS Publications,1996), p. 220.

62 "Teresa Benedict of the Cross Edith Stein." Vatican News Service; Wikipedia, s.v. "Edith Stein," accessed August, 30, 2020, https://en.wikipedia.org/wiki/Edith_Stein.

63 E. Joanne Angelo, "A Special Word to Women Who Have Had an Abortion," United States Conference of Catholic Bishops, accessed September 1, 2020, www.usccb.org/issues-and-action/human-life-and-dignity/abortion.

64 Libreria Editrice Vaticana, *Catechism of the Catholic Church,* 2nd ed. (Washington, DC: US Catholic Conference of Bishops, 1997, 2016), p. 446.

65 David Cloutier, "Why Talk About 'Structures of Sin'?" *Public Discourse Journal,* January 28, 2019.

66 Esmat Gabriel, *The Exemplarily Upbringing of the Child: Transformation Stages Toward Perfect Maturity* (PKP, Inc., 2013), pp. 322, 324.

67 Clement of Alexandria, *Miscellaneous Studies,* 6, 2 (SC30, 71) *Scholarship is Help to Faith*; Thomás Spidlík, *Drinking from the Hidden Fountain* (Collegeville, MN: Cistercian Publications, 1994), p. 384.

68 Evagrius of Pontus, *Sentences on Prayer* 479ff. (PG79, 1167ff.), *'Your Will be Done in Me;'* Thomás Spidlík, *Drinking from the Hidden Fountain* (Collegeville, MN: Cistercian Publications, 1994), p. 368.

69 Esmat Gabriel, *The Exemplary Leadership of Pope Kyrillos VI & Pope Shenouda III,* (PKP, Inc.), 213, pp. 263, 264, 265.

70 Ibid, p. 264.

71 Ibid.

[72] Ibid.

[73] Salah's Report, *In Investigations and Dialogues*, https://eldwla.com/arch.

[74] Esmat Gabriel, *The Exemplary Leadership of Pope Kyrillos VI & Pope Shenouda III*, (PKP, Inc.), 213, p. 264.

[75] Thomas à Kempis, *The Imitation of Christ*, (Mineola, NY: Dover Publications, 2003), p. 39.

Other References

Basil of Seleucia. Homily on Mother of God. 6 (PG85, 425ff), She Bore in Her Womb the Bread of Heaven; Thomás Spidlík, Drinking from the Hidden Fountain (Collegeville, MN: Cistercian Publications, 1994), pp. 394–395.

Thomás Spidlík. "On Authors and Texts;" Drinking from the Hidden Fountain (Collegeville, MN: Cistercian Publications, 1994), p. 407.

About the Author

Dr. Esmat M. Gabriel is an educator and a former faculty member of the Department of Psychiatry and Human Behavior at Thomas Jefferson University. His accomplishments are well recognized by leading health organizations and medical schools, including Pennsylvania Hospital of the University of Pennsylvania Health System and Albert Einstein Medical Center. Dr. Gabriel has received numerous  accolades and acknowledgments for his work and patriotism, including the Ronald Reagan presidential Medal of Merit in 1983. He was also the recipient of the Recognition Award bestowed by His Holiness Pope Tawadros II in 2018 for his devoted contribution to establishing the Coptic Orthodox Church in the United States.

Dr. Gabriel was elected to the New York Academy of Sciences and is listed in *Who's Who in Gerontology*. He is a well-published clinical researcher in the field of human behavior and human development. As a coinvestigator of two national research studies, he led a team that carried out experiments and assessments of a class of medications that currently treat anxiety disorder and insomnia.

Dr. Gabriel is a featured speaker in the United States, Canada, and abroad. He is also a guest contributor to Logos TV's *Coptic Civilization* program in America. His publications include *Contemporary Leadership Styles Analysis: The Exemplary Leadership of Pope Kyrillos VI & Pope Shenouda III and The Exemplarily Upbringing of the Child & Transformational Stages Toward Perfect Maturity*. His most recent publication is *The History of the Coptic Orthodox Church in the United States: From the Land of the Pharaohs to the United States of America* (December 2020).

CPSIA information can be obtained
at www.ICGtesting.com
Printed in the USA
BVHW030543100123
655683BV00006B/28

9 781639 6152